Stories of the Life of

MUHAMMAD

—a selection

Stories of the Life of
MUHAMMAD
—a selection

**A compilation from the writings of early
Muslim chronicles**

Abridged and simplified by
JAMSHID MONAJEM

Bahá'í Publishing Trust
New Delhi, India

First Edition - August 1999

ISBN : 81-86953-50-7

BÁHA'Í PUBLISHING TRUST
Báha'í House, 6 Canning Road
New Delhi-110001, India

Laser type setting by Adept Graphics

DEDICATION

Dedicated to the memory of Gamal Rushdy, co-pioneer with me in Ethiopia, without whose efforts this work could not have been produced, and to my dear friend, Hassan Sabri for getting this work through publication, and to my sons and daughters whose generous assistance made the production of this book possible.

ACKNOWLEDGEMENTS

I wish to convey my deepest appreciation to Dr. Jane A. Faily for reading the manuscript and for her encouraging sentiments. I wish to acknowledge my indebtedness to my daughter Shohreh for the special assistance she rendered to the completion of this project. I am also indebted to my daughter Fetneh who did all the laborious task of typing and computerizing the text, an undertaking she repeated several times as corrections, revisions and transliteration symbols demanded. My sincere gratitude to Burhan Zahra'í for his superb and befitting artistic creation appearing on the cover.

CONTENT

PREFACE

The utterances and actions of the Messengers of God cannot be subject to human scrutiny, analysis and criticism when not conforming to human standards and judgment or to their whims and desires. The Scriptures of all religions report incidents of people rebelling against the commandments and teachings of God's Manifestations and blaming them for innovations that disrupt the social order or the traditional routine of everyday life although they are totally free of blame since they only carry out God's commands.

When Moses was commissioned by God to go to Pharaoh to rescue the Israelites from bondage and bring them out of Egypt and to the land promised to Abraham, Isaac and Jacob, his main adversary was the ruler of Egypt, but the treatment accorded to him by the very people he had come to save was not less painful. They constantly nagged and complained. When Pharaoh cut off their supply of straw and they could not produce as many bricks as they had done therefore, and were flogged in consequence, accused of laziness, they laid the blame on Moses, saying, 'May this bring the Lord's judgment down upon you: you have made us stink in the nostrils of Pharaoh and his subjects: you have put a sword in their hands to kill us.' (Exod. 5: 20-22) When in dread of the Egyptian forces pursuing them, they reproached Moses, saying, 'Were there no graves in Egypt, that you should have brought us here to die in the wilderness? See what you have done to us by bringing us out of Egypt! Is not this just what we meant when we said in Egypt, "Leave us alone; let us be slaves of the Egyptians?" We would rather be slaves to the Egyptians than die in the wilderness.' (Exod. 14: 11-12) When in the wilderness of Sinai they experienced shortage of food and water, they complained to Moses, saying, 'If only we had died at the Lord's hand in Egypt, where we sat round the fleshpots and had plenty of bread of eat! But you have brought us out into the wilderness to let this whole assembly starve to death.' (Exod. 16: 2-3) And when they said 'Give us water to drink,' Moses said, 'Why do you dispute with me? Why do you challenge the Lord?' There the people became so thirsty that they raised an outcry against Moses: "Why have you brought us out of Egypt with our children and herds to let us all die of thirst?" Moses cried to the Lord, "What shall I do with these people? In a moment they will be stoning me."...' (Exod. 17: 2-4)

Such instances in the life of Moses, as reported in the Torah, are too numerous to be quoted in this brief tract. They are, however, sufficient to indicate that at the advent of a Manifestation of God, the tide of change sweeping over humanity is so alarming and man's inability to comprehend the future blessings and beneficial consequences of such a change so blinding, so confusing that he accuses and rebels against the Messenger ignoring his plea that he is only the bearer of a message, the transmitter of God's Will to mankind and that he is compelled to strictly obey the behests of the Supreme Universal Spirit. 'Go now,' said God to Moses when he told Him that he was slow and hesitant of speech, I will help your speech and tell you what to say.' (Exod. 4: 12)

Similar happenings are reported in the Gospels. When some of John's disciples fell into dispute with the Jews on the issue of purification, they came to John who told them: 'He who comes from heaven bears witness to what he has seen and heard, yet no one accepts his witness. To accept his witness is to attest that God speaks the truth; for he whom God sent utters the words of God, so measureless is God's gift of the Spirit.' (St. John 3: 34) When the Jews determined to kill Jesus, not only for breaking the Sabbath, but also for 'calling God his own Father thus claiming equality with God,' he refuted the charge, replying, 'In truth, in very truth I tell you, the Son can do nothing by himself, he does only what he sees the Father doing: What the Father does, the Son does...' And later, 'I cannot act by myself: I judge as I am bidden, and my sentence is just, because my aim is not my own will, but the will of him who sent me.' (St. John 5: 19, 30) Again, 'But he who sent me speaks the truth, and what I heard from him I report to the world... I do nothing on my own authority, but in all that I say, I have been taught by my father. He who sent me is present with me, and has not left me (St. John 8: 26-28) And yet again, '...I am not myself the source of the words I speak to you: it is the Father who dwells in me doing his own work.' (St. John 14: 10) And finally, 'I do not speak on my own authority, but the Father who sent me has himself commanded me what to say and how to speak. I know that his commands are eternal life. What the Father has said to me, therefore — that is what I speak.' (Ibid 12: 49-50)

Like verses have been revealed in the Qur'án. 'But when our clear signs are recited to them, they who look not forward to meeting Us, say, "Bring a different Qur'án from this, or make some change in it." Say: it is not for me to change it as mine own soul prompteth. I follow only what is revealed to me. Verily, I fear, if I rebel against my Lord, the punishment of a great day.' (Q. 10 :15) 'Perhaps thou wilt suppress a part of what hath been revealed to thee, and will be distressed at heart lest they say, "If a treasure be not sent down to him, or an angel come with him..." But thou art only a warner, and God hath all things in His charge. (Q. 11 : 12) 'Say: In sooth I am only a man like you. It hath been revealed to me that your God is one only God...' (Q. 18 : 110) 'O Prophet fear thou God, and obey not the unbelievers and the hypocrites; Truly God is Knowing, Wise: but follow what is revealed to thee from thy Lord: cognisant truly is He of all your actions...' (Q. 22 : 1-2) 'Say: I only warn you of what hath been revealed to me; but the deaf will not hear the call, whenever they are warned.' (Q. 21 : 45) And there are more, far more, but aren't these sufficient proof that the Messengers of God are blameless and the embodiment of innocence since they are obedient to God's every command.

And Baháu'lláh was no exception in this regard. Addressing the Sháh of Persia, the tyrant Nasiri'd-Din Sháh, he wrote: 'O king! I was but a man like others, asleep upon my couch, when lo, the breezes of the All-Glorious were wafted over Me and taught Me the knowledge of all that hath been. This thing is not from Me, but from One Who is Almighty and All-Knowing. And He bade Me lift up My voice between earth and heaven, and for this there befell Me what hath caused the tears of every man of understanding to flow. The learning current amongst men I studied not; their schools I entered not. Ask of the city wherein I dwelt, that thou mayest be well assured that I am not of them who speak falsely. This is but a leaf which the winds of the will of thy Lord, the Almighty, the All-Praised have stirred. Can it be still when the tempestuous winds are blowing? Nay, by Him Who is the Lord of all Names and Attributes! They move it as they list. The evanescent is as nothing before Him Who is the Ever-Abiding. His all-compelling summons hath reached Me, and caused Me to speak His praise amidst all people. I was indeed as one dead when His behest was uttered. The hand of the will of thy Lord, the Compassionate, the Merciful, transformed Me. Can anyone speak forth of his own accord that for which all men, both high and low, will protest against him? Nay, by Him Who taught the Pen the eternal mysteries, save him whom the grace of the Almighty, the All-Powerful, hath strengthened. The Pen of the Most High addreseth Me saying: Fear not. Relate unto His Majesty, the Sháh that which befell thee. His heart, verily, is between the fingers of thy Lord, the God of Mercy, that haply the sun of justice and bounty may shine forth above the horizon of his heart. Thus hath the decree been irrevocably fixed by Him Who is the All-Wise.' cited in 'The Bahá'í Revelation,' pp. 26/7.

How happy, how tranquil, how prosperous and fruitful the world would be if humanity would only follow the Manifestations in utter servitude and obedience to the behests of the Almighty.

INTRODUCTION

The stories that follow have been gleaned from two important sources: Muhammad ibn-Ishaq's 'Sirat Rasul Alláh', translated by A. Guillaúme, and Tabari's 'Tarikh al-Rusul w-al-Muluk, vols. VI, VII, and IX which relate to Muhammad's life and time, translated by several scholars under the supervision of an Editorial Board and printed at the State University of New York Press.

The narratives are intended to give the reader, on the one hand, a glimpse of life in 'Arabia before the advent of the Apostle of God — the superstitious beliefs and practices that were prevalent in that land, the people's inordinate pride and reverence of lineage, excessive loyalty to one's clan, their crude manners, total absence of central administration[1] and machinery for the execution of justice — and, on the other, the incredibly rapid transformation that took place in the moral, political, economic and cultural life of the people as a result of Muhammad's unwavering adherence to truth, His teaching efforts and the laws and ordinances that He enacted in the course of twenty-three years of his ministry — The impulse He generated in a people, uncouth, uncultivated, and superstitious, an irresistible force that uplifted them, in a short span of time, to heights of learning and civilization staggers the imagination, and is clear proof of the power latent in the Word of God and its impelling force on man's mind and heart.

---

[1] Sayyid Ameer'Alí in his book, 'The Spirit of Islám', pp. 5-7 states that in the city of Makkah there existed a governing body consisting of ten Sharifs (noblemen) "These decemvirs occupied the first place in the States and their offices were hereditary in favour of the eldest member or chief of each family." He then gives the function, the designation, the rank and the name of the family or clan holding each of the ten offices.

The stories are presented in abridged form. Whenever conflicting reports appear in the original texts or several informats describe the events with only minor changes, only one report has been selected and presented in the simplest language.

Family names had not come into use at the time. To distinguish between two or more same names, the geneology of the person, usually up to great-grandfather, was used. At times this practice was extended to remoter forefathers. Thus Ibn Ishaq writes: 'Abdullah b. al-Zibrára b. 'Adiy b. Qays b. 'Adiy b. Sa'd b. Sahm b. 'Amr b. Husays b. Ka'b b. lu'ayy b. Ghalib b. Fihr said... ' (Sira, p. 28) ('b.' is the abbreviation of 'ibn' which means 'son of'). Although mentioning names of a person's forefathers to the 12th ancestry was most unusual, stating names of three or four forebears was common, a practice which renders the story dull and uninteresting particularly to a Western reader unfamiliar with foreign names. Furthermore, the reader cannot make a mental or emotional bond with names of people who lived over 1400 years ago, be they 'Alí, Hasan, 'Abdullah or whatever. It is the story that ought to engage his/her interest. So, only first names have been used except when confusion could be avoided by the mention of the father's name, too.

A large amount of poetry is inserted in ibn Ishaq's 'Sira'. Arabs paid tribute to their dead and eulogized their heroes in lengthy elegies and odes. The fallen in the campaigns were mourned by friends and satirized by foes in verse. Acts of valour in combats received high praise in poetic compositions. These have been totally eliminated. Although they are often entertaining, their insertion in this compilation serves no useful purpose.

It is befitting to give a brief introduction to the authors and their books.

Muhammad ibn-Ishaq was born in Madinah in A.H. 85 (A.D. 704). He followed his father's footsteps, pursuing a career of research and scholarship. The object of his quest was the life and wars of Muhammad, the Apostle of God. His keen interest in collecting material on this subject took him to Egypt were he attended the lectures of renowned scholars on traditions. He returned to Madinah and collected more data from second generation believers whose fathers, uncles or aunts had been closely associated with the Apostle, His wives 'A'isha and Hafsa, His immediate companions 'Alí, Abu Bakr, 'Umar and others. He was soon recognized as an authority not only on history and tradition but also on the Qur'án and Islamic law. Al-Zuhri, himself a notable scholar "is reported to have said that Medina would never lack 'ilm (learning) as long as Ibn-Ishaq was there, and he eagerly gathered from him the details of the prophet's wars."[2] But soon he found himself the centre of a hot controversy over his lost book of Sunan[3] which aroused the enmity of Malik ibn-Anas the author of the Madinah school of Islamic law, was accused of being a Qadari and a Shi'ah, and left the city. He stayed in Kufa, al-Jazirah[4], and Ray[5], residing finally in Baghdád, where he died in A.H. 151 (A.D. 767/8). A few copies were made of his 'Sirat Rasul Allah by his pupils in Ray. The only copy extant is the recension of Ibn-Hisham, translated by A. Guillaume, and the main source of the stories in this compilation.

No chronicle can claim perfect accuracy[6]. What is reported or recorded is not always the truth. Even at the present time,

---

[2] A. Guillaúme's Introduction to the 'Sira', p. XIII.

[3] The word means customary practices, traditional usage, norm. The book is lost.

[4] The northern province of Mesopotamia.

[5] A town a short distance south of the present city of Tihrán, capital of Írán.

[6] The only exception to this assertion are the Revelations of God transmitted to mankind through His Messenger as well as the interpretations of Authorized interpreters. The Messenger of God is the bearer of truth and can never be wrong.

and in the most progressive societies where freedom of the press and of expression is an uncontested right, and despite the use of high-tech means of communication, the reporting of events is occasionally tainted to serve special interests and documents are often tampered with or shredded to cover up matters — be the intent self-serving, guarding real or imaginary national security, or benevolent sin-covering. Intentional or inadvertent, misrepresentation of facts is yet another factor making it difficult to come to correct conclusions. Many other devious motivations in handling events, documenting and preserving them, obviously hinder the attainment of truth. At the time of Muhammad when the great majority of the people were illiterate and writing materials extremely scarce in Arabia, events were normally transmitted from mouth to mouth, from generation to generation. Man's natural inclination to overstate events with every such transmission and the tendency to mystify happenings to enhance their importance made it difficult for historians to give an accurate account of events even though, as was the case with Ibn-Ishaq, they interrogated many sources scrupulously, sifted their material carefully, recorded their findings honestly and fairly and were cautious to refrain from personal comments. When in doubt about the veracity of a report Ibn-Ishaq usually resorts to expressions such as 'he (they) allege', 'as he (they) informed me', and more frequently 'only God knows the truth', implying that the reported incident in his opinion is far-fetched and unbelievable. Much of what he chronicled, however, can be considered fairly reliable inasmuch as he collected his materials from numerous trustworthy informants. One must also consider that the 'Sira' has come to be one of the most important sources of material for later Muslim historians, such as the renowned Tabari, and more recently for Western historians of Islám. In his monumental book, Tabari acknowledges that Ibn-Ishaq is a most reliable source of historical material. Most probably he used one of the copies made at Ray, now lost, judging by discrepancies observable in his version and Ibn-Hisham's recension.

Tabari was born in Tabaristan, a northern province of Írán, south of the Caspian Sea, in A.D. 838/9. He ranks among the foremost Muslim historians. His 'Tarikh al-Rusul w-al-Muluk, translated into 38 volumes and titled *The History of al-Tabari*, covers the period from the creation of the world to A.D. 915, and has served as source material for many later Muslim historians. His 'Jami' al-Bayan fi Tafsir al Qur'án, 30 volumes, is the largest commentary on the Qur'án and one of the richest collections of traditions. In his search for learning he travelled throughout Persia, al-'Iráq, Syria and Egypt, often in great poverty. "On one occasion he was forced to sell the sleeves of his shirt to buy bread for sustenance. An idea of his industry and enthusiasm for learning may be gained from the popular tradition that during forty years al-Tabari wrote forty sheets every day."[7]

The stories that follow are extracted chiefly from Ibn-Ishaq's 'Sira, while volumes VI, VII and IX relating to Muhammad's life and time were closely examined to supply the reader with as much reliable information as possible. Unfortunately Vol. VIII of 'Tarikh al-Tabari' is still unavailable and could not be consulted.

---

[7] Cited by Philip K, Hitti in his 'History of the Arabs', 10th Edition, p. 391.

ABDULLAH
A SACRIFICE TO ALLÁH

'Abdullah, Muhammad's father, was the youngest son of 'Abdu'l-Muttalib. It is related that 'Abdu'l-Muttalib had vowed that if Alláh would grant him ten sons who would protect him in his old age, he would sacrifice one to Him at the Ka'bah. When his wish was granted, he called his sons and told them of his vow desiring them to respect it. They consented. So, 'Abdu'l-Muttalib asked each of his sons to write his name on an arrow, and took these before Hubal[8], that was the most revered idol of the Makkans, and whose statue was placed by a well in the middle of the Ka'bah. He gave them to the man who cast the lots[9], asking him to cast the lots for his sons. It was 'Abdullah's arrow that came out.

Taking a large, sharp knife, 'Abdu'l-Muttalib led his youngest son to Isa'f and Na'ila[10] to sacrifice him. His sons and several of the notables of the Quraysh appealed to him to "offer the highest expiatory sacrifice for him", lest his action

---

[8] Hubal, along with all other idols existing in the Ka'bah, was destroyed by Muhammad at His conquest of Makkah in A.H. 8.

[9] The Arabs in pre-Islamic times had a custom of casting lots by arrows (Zalem) when in doubt about the correctness or the wisdom of a decision, such as a marriage, the proper date for the circumcision of a son, embarking on a journey, digging a well for water, etc. They took the affair to Hubal with a fee, sometimes as much as a hundred dirhams and a slaughter camel, for final decision by the arrows. Divination by arrows was prohibited in the Qur'án (Q. 5:3).

[10] It is related that when Jurhum assumed the custodianship of the Ka'bah, they acted unlawfully, embezzling gifts and donations to the Ka'bah, dealing unjustly with visitors to the Ka'bah, and even fornicating within it. Isa'f fornicated with Na'ilah inside the Ka'bah and they were turned into two stones at which location the Quraysh used to slaughter their sacrifices. T 1076 and 1132.

may become a precedent for others to scarifice their sons. They even agreed to pay any amount, even their whole property to redeem the young man. So, it was agreed that 'Abdu'l-Muttalib should consult a sorceress who lived in Híjáz.He rode with his son to Ya<u>th</u>rib, only to find that she had gone to <u>Kh</u>aybar. They rode on to <u>Kh</u>aybar. The sorceress asked them to wait in that town until her familiar spirit visited her. Later she informed them that she had received news of her spirit and asked them how much was blood-money among them. "Ten camels", they answered. She told 'Abdu'l-Muttalib to take 'Abdullah and ten camels to Hubal and cast lots between the two. "If the lot falls against the camels", she said, "then sacrifice them in his stead, for your lord will be satisfied and your client escape death. If, however, it falls against the young man, add ten more camels and repeat it until your Lord is satisfied."

'Abdu'l-Muttalib then returned to Makkah and did as was instructed. They cast lots and the arrow fell against 'Abdullah not once, not twice but until there were one hundred camels, when, finally, the lot fell against the camels. The Quray<u>sh</u> were jubilant, but not 'Abdu'l-Muttalib who said, "No, by Alláh, not until I cast lots three times." Then the casting of the lots continued, but each time the arrow fell against the camels. They were then slaughtered and the poor people of Makkah feasted over their meat, and thanked Alláh for saving 'Abdullah's life.

MUHAMMAD'S BIRTH AND CHILDHOOD

'Abdullah was married to Aminah, daughter of Wahb b. 'Abdu Manaf, a chieftain of B. Zuhrah. Aminah was a woman of noble birth, highly respected among the Quraysh. The marriage was consummated immediately after the wedding and she conceived the Messenger of God. But 'Abdullah died before his son was born. He became ill when returning from Syria in a Quraysh caravan, halted in Yathrib and stayed there until his death, which occured a few months before the birth of his son. Aminah gave birth to a son and called him Muhammad. This was on a Monday in the year of the Elephant, A.D. 570 or 571[11]. Rumour spread among the Makkans (the truth of which is uncertain) that during her pregnancy Aminah said she heard a voice telling her: "You are pregnant with the Lord of this people. When he is born say, 'I put him in the care of the One from the evil of every envier: then call him Muhammad'." Also that she saw a light come forth from her by which she could see the castles of Busra in Syria.

'Abdu'l-Muttalib was soon informed of the birth of the new child. It is said that he took him before Hubal in the Ka'bah, prayed to Alláh and thanked Him for His gift. Then they chose Halimah and asked her to suckle him.

Now listen to Halimah's narrative: It was a year of famine. The land was parched and the yield was poor for it had not rained for a long time. Times were hard, people were poverty-

---

[11] Muslim historians agree on this date, Monday 12th Rabi-ul-Awwal of the first year of the Era of the Elephant, coinciding with the 40th year of the reign of Chosroes Anuishirwan. Western historians calculate the date variantly August 20th A.D. 570 and April 20th A.D. 571.

stricken and could not make ends meet. My husband, my child whom I was nursing and myself joined several other families who were leaving their country in search of some income to reduce their suffering. I was riding a she-donkey and we had a she-camel that gave not a drop of milk. My child cried the whole night from hunger as my own milk was insufficient. When we reached Makkah, the women in our company refused Aminah's newly-born son as everyone said, "An orphan! What hope do we have to get payment from his father?" I, too, did not accept him at first. But then out of compassion for the bereaved mother and the fatherless child I said to my husband: "I hate to return home without a suckling. Let us take that orphan." "Do as you please," he replied, "perhaps Alláh will bless us on his account."

So we took the baby boy, and as soon as I held him in my bosom, my breasts overflowed with milk. So abundant was the milk that both he and my own son had their fill and were satisfied. My husband got up and went to tend our she-camel, and Lo and behold, her udders were full. We drank all the milk we desired and were satisfied. We all enjoyed a sound sleep that night after long sleepless nights. My husband said to me, "Do you know, Halimah, you have surely taken a blessed child!" We set out the next day. I carried the baby riding my she-donkey. She took off so swiftly that the other donkeys could not keep pace with her. The women in our company were certainly surprised. " Confound you, woman! Slow down so we can catch up with you. Is this the same donkey you rode to Makkah?" "Sure it is," I said. "By Alláh! It is a miracle the way it is galloping."

At last we reached our home in Bani Sa'd country. During the time the boy was with us our flock gave abundant milk while the flocks of our neighbours were almost dry. The boy grew strong and lusty. When he reached the age of two, I weaned him and took him back to his mother. We had enjoyed Alláh's blessings during the little boy's stay with us so much that we were loath to let him go and appealed to Aminah to let us keep him rather than expose him to the pest in Makkah. We persisted in our plea until she let us take him back with us.

A few months later, our son and his foster brother were playing with our lambs behind our tent, when our son came running and shouting, "Two men in white clothes threw Muhammad down, opened up his belly and are stirring it up." We ran out and found him standing up looking dazed and haggard. We asked Muhammad what had happened. He repeated his foster brother's story. My husband thought the boy had a stroke and should be taken back to his mother. Reluctantly we did that and, upon her questioning, we explained all that had happened.

Here Halimah's story ends. But other reports regarding this incident allege that the Prophet years later, when asked by some of His companions about His early life, said, "... while I was with a brother of mine behind our tents shepherding the lambs, two men in white raiment came to me with a gold basin full of snow. Then they seized me and opened up my belly, extracted my heart and split it; then they extracted a black drop from it and threw it away; then they washed my heart and my belly with that snow until they had thoroughly cleaned them. Then one said to the other, weigh him against ten of his people; they did so and I outweighed them. Then they weighed me against a hundred and then a thousand, and I outweighed them. He said, "Leave him alone, for by Alláh, if you weighed him against all his people he would outweigh them."[12]

---

[12] Supernatural events have been recorded in the lives of all God's Messengers, such as God's covenant with Abraham concerning circumcision when he was ninety-nine years old (Gen. 17:10-14, 24), and God's promise to him that Sarah, his wife, would He bless with a child upon which he "fell upon his face, and laughed and said in his heart, 'Shall a child be born unto him that is an hundred years old, and shall Sarah that is ninety years old, bear?" (Gen.

When Muhammad was about six years old his mother Aminah died. He was reared by his grandfather 'Abdu'l-Muttalib who loved him more than his own sons and often referred to his great future. Upon his death, he entrusted the youth to Abu Talib since he and Muhammad's father were brothers of the same mother, and he became one of his family.

17: 16, 17); Moses, when only three months old, being put in an ark which was then laid in the flags by the river's brink and found by the king's sister and raised in the palace of the very king who had ordered all the male children born into Israel to be cast into the river; then again His seeing the Burning Bush at Sinai, a signal of His appointment as God's Messenger; Jesus being born of the Holy Spirit and Virgin Mary, and apparently even more incredible is the account of His birth and of His conversation, when still in the cradle, with Mary's relatives who scolded her for giving birth to a child out of wedlock, recounted in the Qur'án (19:22-34); and later when "the heavens were opened unto him, and he saw the Spirit of God descending like a dove, and alighting upon him," (Matt. 3:16) an intimation of His appointment as a Messenger of God; the episode of the Báb's martyrdom (see G.P.B. pp. 52-57); Bahá'u'lláh's dream, when a child of five or six years, that, while walking in the garden, He was attacked by huge birds flying overhead but they could not harm Him; then He went to bathe in the sea, and there He was attacked by fishes but they did Him no harm. An interpreter of dreams told Bahá'u'lláh's father that the sea was this world and the birds and fishes represented the peoples of the world who would assail Him because He would announce a great doctrine but they would be powerless to harm Him and in the end, He would triumph over them all. Bahá'u'lláh's experience in the Siyah Chal (the Black Pit) of Tihrán, when He saw in a vision a maiden suspended betwixt heaven and earth, and, pointing her finger to His head, called all the dwellers of both heaven and earth, saying, "By God! This is the Best-Beloved of the worlds, and yet ye comprehend not..." (Bahá'u'lláh, the king of Glory, p. 82). In the story of Muhammad as in most of the other incidents mentioned above, the true significances are: (1) God purifies the hearts of his Messengers and they are absolutely free from sin and error. They are the embodiment of truth; (2) that God doth what He pleaseth, and no power can frustrate His purpose; (3) that the Messenger of God outweighs the forces of opposition, despite all apparent material setbacks; and (4) that the Manifestations of God receive intimation of their appointment in symbolic ways.

THE MEETING WITH THE MONK BAHIRA

The prominent people of Makkah were wealthy merchants. They organized two caravans annually. One to the south where they bought frankincense, a sweet-smelling resinous substance which was obtained from a tree that grew there, and spices that came from India. The other northward to Syria where they disposed of their goods and returned with other merchandise to Makkah. The caravan to the north was an elaborate affair consisting at times of some thouand camels, a large number of horse-men and of course a number of attendants to lower the packs at resting stations and load the camels when setting out on the day's journey as well as to tend to the animals.

Abu Talib joined a merchant caravan to Syria one year and took Muhammad, then about twelve years old, with him. A Christian monk, named Bahira, lived in a cell in Busra (Bostra), a station on the 'spice-Road' to Syria. He was well-versed with Prophecy and from a book in his possession had learnt the signs portending the coming of a messenger of God. When caravans arrived at Busra, he usually kept to his cell and paid little or no attention to them. But when Abu Talib's caravan approached, he recognized that a cloud overshadowed the young boy and kept moving with him protecting him from the scorching sun. When Bahira saw that, he left his cell and invited the people to a meal he had prepared for them. During the meal, he observed Muhammad intently and found in his features and manners what corresponded with the description in his book. When the meal was over and the people had gone, he approached Muhammad and asked him about what happened during his waking and his sleep and his attitude towards problems generally. Muhammad's replies coincided remarkably with the description in his book. Finally, he looked at Muhammad's back and found the seal of prophethood between his shoulders.

The monk then told Abu Talib of the great future of his nephew: "Take your nephew back to his country and guard him carefully against the Jews, for by Alláh! if they see him and know about him what I know, they will do him evil; a great future lies before this nephew of yours, so take him home quickly." So Abu Talib finished his business in Syria as quickly as he could and returned home with his precious charge.

HOW GOD
PROTECTED MUHAMMAD FROM
EVIL PRACTICES

It was related from 'Alí b. Abu Talib: "I heard the Apostle say, 'Twice I was tempted to do what the people in the pagan days used to do, and both times Alláh guarded me. Once I asked the young boy who was shepherding with me to look after my flock for me while I spent the night in Makkah as young men did. He agreed and I went off with that purpose in mind. When I reached the first house in Makkah I heard the sound of tambourines and flutes and asked what was going on. They said that a marriage was taking place. I sat down to watch but soon fell asleep until I was awakened by the touch of the sun. I went back to my friend who asked me what I had done. I told him what had happened. Another night I had a similar experience. After that I was never inclined to evil, right up to the time when Alláh honoured me by appointing me His Messenger'."

MUHAMMAD'S MARRIAGE
TO KHADIJA

Khadija was a noble lady of Quraysh, daughter of Khuwaylid, highly respected in Makkah and much sought after by many suitors. She was a widow, who had been twice married, and inherited a handsome fortune which established her in a fairly good position as a merchant in Makkah. She employed men to engage in trade with her property and paid them a good share of the proceeds. When she heard that Muhammad, a distant relative, was a man of integrity and of good character, dependable and responsible, she sent for him and offered to pay him a larger share of the profits if he would agree to work for her. She also gave him her slave Maysarah to accompany him on his journeys to Syria.

Muhammad accepted her offer. They set out with her merchandise and travelled until they reached Syria. They halted in the shade of a tree near a monk's cell. The monk came out of his cell and asked Maysarah who it was who was resting beneath that yonder tree. "A man of Quraysh", Maysarah replied, "One of the keepers of the Ka'bah". The monk exclaimed, "None but a prophet ever sat beneath this tree".

Muhammad sold the goods, bought merchandise that he judged would sell well in Makkah, and they returned. Maysarah noticed that during the extreme mid-day heat two angels shaded Muhammad as he rode his camel, and reported his observation and the monk's remarks to Khadija when they arrived back in Makkah. The merchandise fetched nearly twice its price. Khadija was elated, sent for Muhammad and proposed marriage. Muhammad accepted her proposal. He and his uncle, Hamza, went to Khuwaylid and asked for her hand, as was the custom at the time. They say that at first K͟huwaylid thought Muhammad was not a proper match for his daughter whose status, dignity and wealth could claim far greater men of Quraysh, but in the end he consented and they were married. Al-Waqidi, however, questions the validity of this report and quotes other sources as saying that her father had died years before and that her uncle 'Amr gave her away to Muhammad. At the time of their marriage he was twenty-five years of age, while she was forty and had born two sons and a daughter to her previous husbands.

K͟hadija was a loving, caring wife who bore her husband all his children, except Ibrahim, altogether three sons and four daughters. The three sons died before Muhammad became a Messenger. The four daughters accepted Islám and emigrated to Madinah. Fátima, 'Alí's consort, alone survived her father. K͟hadija remained Muhammad's only wife until her death at the age of sixty five. She was the first believer, and her Lord's main support and comfort for twenty five years, and particularly in the early days of His ministry when the opposition of the Quraysh was severe, adamant, and often violent. His love and affection for her never flagged. 'A' isha used to say: "I was never so jealous of any one of the Prophet's wives as I was of K͟hadija, although I never saw her. The Prophet was always talking of her, and He would very often slay goats, cut them up, and send pieces of them as presents to K͟hadija's female friends. I often said to Him, 'One might suppose there had not been such another woman as K͟hadija in the world!' And the Prophet would then praise her and say she was so and so, and I had children by her." Another hadith related to the Prophet says: "K͟hadija, Fátima, the Virgin Mary, and Asiyah the wife of Pharaoh, were the four perfect women of history."

MUHAMMAD SETTLED A DISPUTE DURING THE RE-BUILDING OF THE KA'BAH

The treasures of the Ka'bah were kept in a well in the middle of it. The walls surrounding the Ka'bah were made of loose stones to just above a man's height. When it was discovered that part of the treasure was stolen, the Quraysh decided to raise the walls and roof it. This resolution was further strenghthened by the discovery of a merchant ship that had wrecked at Jeddah, sixty miles away, and cast ashore, providing the necessary wood for the roofing as well as by the fact that a Copt who was a carpenter happened to be there at the time. But there was the problem of the snake which lived in the well and sunned itself every day lying on the wall. Every time someone approached, it raised its head, rustled and opened its mouth terrifying the oncomer. One day as the snake was basking in the sun, a large bird swooped down on it and carried it off. The Quraysh took this as a good omen and, confident that their project had now received Alláh's good pleasure, decided to undertake the job forthwith. They also agreed that the money to be spent on the job should come from clean earnings, not from ill-gotten gains, usury, or any act of injustice and violence.

They pulled down the old wall to the foundation and rebuilt a new wall. When they reached the height where the Black Stone was to be lodged, the four clans of Quraysh that had divided the job of the erection of the walls among themselves fell into a dispute, each desiring to have the honour of raising the Black Stone and placing it in its proper place at the exclusion of the others. Operations stopped for four or five days until the oldest man of the Quraysh suggested that the first man who would enter the gate of the Mosque that day should be regarded arbitrator by all parties and settle the dispute. To this suggestion they all agreed. It so happened that Muhammad was the first to come in through the gate. All were happy to see him. They said, "This is the trustworthy one. We are satisfied. This is Muhammad." When he learned of what had happened, he asked for a cloak. They brought him one. He placed the Black Stone inside it with his own hands, and told the tribes to take the sides of the cloak and lift it up together. They did this. When it was lifted to the right height, he took the Black Stone with his own hands and put it in the proper place. This done, the job proceeded with little difficulty until successfully completed. Before he received his mission, Muhammad was called "the trustworthy one" (al-Amin). Five years after the rebuilding of the wall, he received the first Revelation from Alláh.

ARAB SOOTHSAYERS PREDICT THE COMING OF A PROPHET

Have you noticed that with the approach of the springtime there is a perceptible change in the air. The universe suddenly comes to life. The dead trees bud and glow in blossoms. The birds and the bees chirp, warble and buzz, restlessly fly from one branch to another and rejoice in the coming of the springtime. The earth is carpeted with fresh verdure decked with violets, crocuses, daffodils, narcissus and tulip. So is the appearance of a Messenger of God. The old order is found to be defective; habits and mores which form the basis of human relationships seem to be deficient; new ideas and attitudes develop necessitating change. Some men and women are inspired to foretell the advent of a Messenger who will bring about such a change and establish a new order.

In Arabia, there were many soothsayers, male and female, who predicted the coming of a prophet. They told their kinsmen that they had been visited by the Jinn who had overheard such tidings. They kept repeating these premonitions, but the Makkans ignored them until the Messenger of God appeared calling them to Alláh as the only God to be worshipped and not to be associated with any other gods.

A female soothsayer of Bani Sahm was visited by her familiar spirit one night, shrieking:

" I know what I know,
The day of wounding and slaughter."

The Quraysh were puzzled and asked what it meant. The spirit returned, screaming:

"Death, what is death?
In it bones are thrown here and there."

The Qura<u>sh</u> did not understand it until the battles of Badr and Uhud took place and revealed the meaning of the message.

'Umar, the second Caliph, was sitting in the mosque one day when he had an unexpected visitor, one who had been a soothsayer in the days of ignorance, but was now a Muslim. 'Umar wished to know whether the visitor had received any intimations from his familiar spirits when he was a soothsayer. "Yes," said the visitor, "he came to me a month or so before Islám and said:

> Have you considered the jinn and their confusion, their religion a despair and a delusion,
> clinging to their camels' saddle cloths in profusion?"

Then 'Umar related another incident when, about a month or so before the Apostle's Call, he was standing along with a number of others, waiting to get a share of the meat of a calf an Arab was sacrificing, when a sharp, piercing voice came out of the belly of the calf, saying:

> " O blood red one,
> The deed is done,
> A man will cry,
> Beside God none."

The men of <u>Th</u>aqif, a prominent clan residing in al-Ta'if, were the first to see falling stars. They thought they were being flung at them and went to 'Amr, a tribesman known for his sound judgment for explanation. He told them that if the stars were the ones guiding the caravans on land and sailing boats on the seas and made the four seasons, then by Alláh! it meant the end of the world. But if other stars were being cast down, then it augured some purpose which Alláh intended to bring about for mankind.

THE JEWS PREDICT THE ADVENT OF THE APOSTLE OF GOD

The Arabs before Islám believed in Alláh, but worshipped idols, too. The Jews then living in Makkah, Yathrib and Khaybar, had their holy Book, the Torah, and had the knowledge which the Arab polytheists did not possess. For as long as anybody remembered there had been feud between them, and the Jews threatened them, saying, "The time of a prophet to be sent has now come. We will kill you with his aid as 'Ad[13] and Irám[14] perished." When the Apostle came, the idol worshipping Arabs accepted Him; the Jews rejected Him. Then Alláh revealed this verse:

And when a Book came unto them from God,
confirming the Scriptures which were with them,
although they had before prayed for victory over those
who believed not, yet when there came unto them He
of Whom they had knowledge, they disbelieved in Him.
The curse of God on the infidels.

Q. 2:89

Salih recounts the following anecdote: "I was a young boy resting in the courtyard one day when a Jewish neighbour came to visit us. He talked to the family about resurrection, reckoning, balance, paradise and hell. An unbelieving member of the family said scoffingly: 'Do you really believe

---

[13]An ancient Arab tribe who, it is alleged, worshipped four gods — the god of rain, the god of preservation from danger, the god of sustenance and the god restoring health. According to the Qur'án, god sent Hud to this tribe to guide them to the worship of one God.

Q. 11: 50-60

[14]Irám was the region or town where the tribe of Ad lived in Arabia.

Q. 89: 6-8

that the dead will come to life again and will either live in a delectable garden or in a fire according to their deeds?' 'Yes,' said the Jew, 'and by God he would rather be in the hottest oven in his own house.' He then pointed in the direction of Makkah and Yaman and said, 'a prophet will come from that land.' When asked when this would happen, he said, gazing at me, 'This boy will see him if lives a natural life.' and by Alláh! A night and a day had not passed, when the Apostle raised His call. We believed in Him but he denied Him. 'Aren't you the man who made those predictions?' we asked him. 'Sure', he said, 'but this is not the man'."

'Asim relates the story of the conversion of three Jews to Islám in this manner. "A Syrian Jew, Ibn al-Hayyaban came to one of Bani Qurayza in Yathrib before Islám. He was a holy man. In the time of drought, he would pray for rain, and sure enough, it would fall in response to his prayer. This happened on a number of occasions. When he was about to die, he said, 'O Jews, what do you think made me leave a land of bread and wine to come to a land of hardship and hunger?' When we told him that we could not think of a good reason, he said that he had come in anticipation of the coming of a prophet whose time was well nigh, so as to follow him. 'Follow him before others do, O Jews, and let nothing keep you back from him, for he rewards the believers and punishes severely the opposers'."

When later, subsequent to the battle of Badr, the Apostle of Alláh laid siege on B. Qurayza, the three men who, as growing youths, had heard the holy man's predictions, said to the Jews, "This is the prophet whose appearance Ibn al-Hayyaban foretold." They accepted Islám, saved their souls, their families and their property. The rest of the tribe refused to recognize Muhammad as a Messenger of God and perished.

THE STORY OF SALMAN, THE PERSIAN

In the village of Jayy in Isfahan[15], there lived a man who owned a large farm and much property. He had a son, named Salman, whom he loved more than anything else in the whole world, so much so that to protect him from a likely injury he often confined him to his house. Salman was such a devoted Parsi, that he was appointed keeper of the sacred fire in that village.

Now let us listen to Salman tell his own story:

One day while I was going to my father's farm, I passed by a place that I later found was a christian church and was enchanted by the voices I heard. I entered the church and found people praying. I was so pleased with what I saw that I decided to remain there for the rest of the day, despite my father's instruction that I should return quickly as he would be anxious for my safety. I found out later that they were christians, believers of a religion which had its beginnings in Syria. When I returned home, I was chided by my father for being late. We had a heated argument over which of the two religions was better. My father insisted that the religion of one's father was better, and I insisted that christianity was better than our religion. So for fear of what I might do, my father bound me in fetters and imprisoned me in his house.

After a few days, with the help of a servant, I clandestinely arranged with the Christians to help me escape the country and accompany a caravan of Christian merchants on their return journey to Syria. When I arrived in Syria, I was directed

---

[15]Some say he was from Ram-Hurmuz, a town about 55 miles southeast of Ahwaz, in Khuzistan.

to the bishop who accepted my offer to serve him, to learn his religion and to pray with him. But soon, I learnt that the bishop was corrupt. The alms and offerings to the church were not spent for the poor, but enriched his coffers — in fact he had stored seven jars full of silver and gold. When the bishop died, I disclosed his corrupt ways to the people and showed them the place where the jars had been hidden. The people were enraged, stoned his dead body and refused to attend his burial ceremony.

His replacement was a bishop of impeccable character, detached from the world, consecrated to the hereafter, with a heartfull of kindness and compassion. I loved him and served him until when he was about to die, I asked him to refer me to someone he trusted. After much thought, he entrusted me to the bishop of Mosul, whom I served for a short time as he, too, was nearing his death. He, in turn, recommended that after his death I should serve a man in Nasibin. I stayed with this kind man in Nasibin for some time. Upon his death, he suggested that I commit myself to a colleague of his in 'Ammuriya. I stayed with him and worked hard. I saved some money and was able to buy a few cows and a flock of sheep. When about to die, he told me that he could not recommend me to anyone who followed in his ways, but that a prophet would soon arise in Arabia in the tradition of Abraham and would migrate to a country where palms grew. Tokens of his prophethood were that he did not eat alms offerings and that between his shoulders was the seal of prophethood. He suggested that I travel to that country if I had the means to do so.

When he died and was buried, I continued living in 'Ammuriya until a caravan of kalbite merchants agreed to take me with them to Arabia in exchange for the cows and the sheep I owned. At Wadi'l-Qura, they sold me to a Jew as a slave. Where was I? I did not know, but the lay of the land and the palm trees reminded me of the description given by the bishop at 'Ammuriya. This gave me hope, but no assurance. Soon a cousin of my recent master visited us, bought me and took me to Yathrib. The prophet was still in Makkah. Then one day as I was on top of a palm tree doing chores, while my master sat below, his cousin approached and said. "Cursed be the B. Qayla! They have gathered in Quba around a man who has come from Makkah and claims to be a prophet."

When I overheard this, it was as though my knees buckled under me and I was about to fall on my master. With difficulty I gained control of myself and came down the palm tree. That evening, I took a bundle of food and took it to the Apostle in Quba: "I have heard that you are trustworthy," I told the Apostle, "and that your companions are in need. I have brought you some food and wish to offer it as alms, as you are more deserving of this." The Apostle thanked me, called a few in his company and said, "Eat!" but he himself refrained from touching the food. So, the first sign described to me by the bishop of Ammuriya was verified. Then a little later, I met the Apostle in the cemetery of Madinah, on the occasion of the burial of one of his companions. I saluted him and, as he was seated, went round to look at his back. The Apostle knew my intention, for he threw off his cloak, and I saw the seal of Prophethood between his shoulders. I knelt and kissed it, weeping unrestrainedly. The Apostle lovingly called me to himself. I told him my story. He wanted his companions to hear it, too.

Service to my master prevented me from joining the Apostle in the battles of Badr and Uhud. Then one day the Prophet called me and commanded me to write a contract agreeing to plant three hundred palm trees for my master in addition to a payment of forty okes of gold against my freedom. I got busy digging the three hundred holes, the companions contributed the palm shoots and the Apostle planted them with his own hands. And would you believe it? Not one of them died! The Apostle then gave me a piece of gold as large as a hen's egg, which had been given to him from a nearby mine. "Take it," said the Prophet, Alláh will pay your debt with it." and so He did, for it weighed exactly forty okes. I was now a free man, and was able later to join the Prophet in the battle of the Trench.

Salman was one of three persons held closest by the Messenger of God. The other two were Abu Dharr, the shepherd, and Miqdad.

FOUR MEN RECOGNIZE THE ABSURDITY OF IDOL WORSHIP

The Quraysh gathered one day each year on a feast day to pay homage to and to circle around the idol to which they offered their sacrifices. During one of these celebrations, four men separated themselves from the rest as they had recognized that the Quraysh had indeed corrupted the religion of Abraham and were following foolish and meaningless practices. These were Waraqa ibn Naufal, 'Ubaydullah ibn Jahsh, 'Uthman ibn al-Huwayrith, and Zayd b 'Amr. They were known as the Hanif or the followers of the religion of Abraham.

Waraqa studied the Christian scriptures. He was Khadija's cousin and, in the early years of the Prophet's mission, urged her to believe in and support Him.

'Ubaydullah continued seeking the truth until the Prophet summoned the people to Islám. He, his wife, Umm Habiba, were among the Muslims who emigrated to Abyssinia. He was converted to Christianity, and died there. The Messenger of God married his widow Umm Habiba.

'Uthman, too, became a Christian and was given a respectable position by the Byzantine emperor.

Zayd ibn 'Amr withdrew from idol worship, and "abstained from meats offered to idols, and from blood and from things strangled." He reproached the Quraysh openly for their evil practices, especially the killing of their infant daughters. He did not espouse Judaism or Christianity and declared that he worshipped the God of Abraham. The following account given by 'Amir b. Rabi'a, cited by Tabari, is quoted verbatim:

I heard Zayd ibn 'Amr ... saying, "I expect a prophet from the descendants of Ishmael, in particular from the descendants of 'Abd al-Muttalib. I do not think that I shall live to see him, but I believe in him, proclaim the truth of his message, and testify that he is a prophet. If you live long enough to see him, give him my greetings. I shall inform you of his description, so that he will not be hidden from you." I said, "Tell me then," and he said, "He is a man who is neither short nor tall, whose hair is neither abundant nor sparse, whose eyes are always red, and who has the seal of prophethood between his shoulders. His name is Ahmad, and this town is his birthplace and the place in which he will commence his mission. Then his people will drive him out and hate the message which he brings, and he will emigrate to Yathrib and triumph. Beware lest you fail to recognize him. I have travelled around every land in search of the faith of Abraham. Every person whom I ask, whether Jew, Christian, or Magian, says, This faith lies where you have come from, and they describe him as I have described him to you. They say that no prophet remains but he." 'Amr said, "When I became a Muslim, I told the Messenger of God what Zayd ibn 'Amr had said, and I gave Him his greetings. He returned his greetings and said, 'May God have mercy on his soul. I saw him in paradise dressed in flowing robes'."

THE EARLIEST REVELATIONS

Several accounts have come to us concerning the manner in which Muhammad received the mantle of Prophethood and was honoured to be the Messenger of God. Trivial are the differences, they agree in substance.

Muhammad loved to be alone with his own soul. For a month every year, he lived a quiet, solitary life at Hira', a mountain near Makkah, in meditation and devotion, feeding the poor with the meagre provision he took with him for his subsistence.

In the fortieth year of his life, during one of these seclusions, while standing one day, he had a strange and an unexpected Revelation. He heard a voice, calling: "Muhammad, I am Alláh, and you are My Messenger!" Terror-stricken, he fell on his knees, trembling. Now Muhammad despised poets and men possessed, and now wondered: "Am I a poet, or a man possessed? The Quraysh should never lay such a stigma on me. Better it is for me to throw myself from the top of the mountain and perish than to endure such reproach." When he was midway to the top of the mountain, he saw a figure standing on the horizon, calling, "O Muhammad! You are the Apostle of Alláh, and I am Gabriel." He turned his face to the left and to the right, but whichsoever side he turned, he saw Gabriel with feet astride the horizon voicing the same words.[16]

In utter fear and confusion, Muhammad hurried home to His wife Khadija and said, "Wrap me up, wrap me up!" Khadija comforted him and assured him that Alláh would never hurt

---

[16]Compare with the descent of the "Most Great Spirit" "Personated by a 'Maiden' to the agonized soul of Baháu'lláh in the Síyáh- Chál of Tehran as described by Himself.   *God Passes By* p. 101

a man so trustworthy, truthful, kind and of such noble character. She went to Waraqa, her cousin, one of the four men of Quráy<u>sh</u> who were expecting the advent of a Messenger of Alláh, and told him what had happened to her husband. Waraqa was overjoyed at the news and assured her that Muhammad was indeed the Prophet of his people, that he should be patient and steadfast as he would assuredly meet great opposition from the Quray<u>sh</u>. He also declared to her that if he lived to see that day, he would assist her husband with dedication and devotion.

It was the month of Ramadan and Muhammad retired to his usual retreat on Hira. Gabriel then appeared to him in a dream. He had with him a sheet of brocade material on which were some writings. "Recite!"[17] He said to Muhammad. "What shall I recite?"[18] was the answer. Gabriel pressed on Muhammad's breast so hard that he thought he would die. Then releasing the pressure, he said again, "Recite!" and Muhammad repeated "What shall I recite?" This was repeated three times. At last Gabriel said:

> Recite thou, in the name of thy Lord, Who created;
> Created man from clots of blood.
> Recite thou! For thy Lord is the most Beneficent,
> Who hath taught the use of the pen;
> Hath taught Man that which he knoweth not.[19]

When Muhammad awoke, it was as though the words were indelibly inscribed in his breast. He was now the Messenger of God.

For a time no other Revelations came to Him. He was distressed and grieved. This period of anxiety lasted for some

---

[17] The Arabic word 'Iqra' can be translated 'Read' or 'recite'.

[18] The sentence 'ma aqra'u' can mean "What shall I read or recite?" or "I cannot read or recite."

[19] Qur'án, Surah 96: 1-5 Rodwell's translation.

time. However, the influence of His words and of His character was so great that some forty of His kinsmen and associates believed in him and his Message. Thereafter Revelations came to him uninterruptedly for twenty years both during His ten years in Makkah and ten years in Madinah. The first Revelation after the Fitrat[20] was Sura 74, the first few verses of which are:

O Thou, enwrapped in thy mantle!
Arise and Warn!
Thy Lord — magnify Him!
Thy raiment — purify it!
The abomination — flee it.

Thus Islám's short period of obscurity ended, and Muhammad was commanded to arise and proclaim the Faith openly. In a later Revelation, Alláh shows His favour to His Messenger and assures him that He is well-pleased with him:

Sura 93 : 1-5

By the noon-day brightness,
and by the night when it darkeneth!
Thy lord hath not foresaken thee, neither hath He been displeased. And surely the future shall be better for thee than the past, and in the end shall thy Lord be bounteous to thee and thou be satisfied.

The first person to believe in the Apostle of Alláh was His wife <u>Kh</u>adija. The first male to believe in him, pray with him and wholeheartedly and unreservedly obey his behests was His cousin 'Alí whom he had fostered in his own household and was to become his son-in-law, the fourth Caliph of Islám, and the 1st Imám of the Shi'ahs, known to them as the 'Commander of the Faithful'.

---

[20] The interval of three years during which Revelation did not come.

THE PROPHET'S DREAM

The Prophet had a dream which the Quraysh interpreted literally, when it was recounted to them, made little sense of it and disputed with Him and scoffed at Him. This occasioned the revelation of the Sura 'The Star', by which God confirms the truth of the Apostle's vision, and declares him to be unerring, uttering nothing from mere impulse but what has been revealed to him by One Mighty, Powerful, and Wise. "Will ye therefore dispute with him concerning that which he saw?" are God's reproachful challenge.

Q. 53 : 12

Now the dream, as reported by a number of early believers, runs something like this:

While the Prophet slept around the Ka'bah, as did many of the Quraysh, at that time, two angels came to him in a dream one night. One said to the other, "Which of the Quraysh have we been ordered to visit?" "We were ordered to meet their chief," responded the other. Then they left, but soon returned with a third angel. They turned the Prophet over on His back, opened His breast and with the water of Zamzam washed away all doubt about the truthfulness of idol-worship, and the traditional beliefs and practices of pre-Islamic Era. Then they filled His breast with faith and wisdom, which they carried in a golden vessel, and carried him up to heaven. After the gatekeeper made sure that Muhammad's Mission had begun, he admitted them. In the first heaven, Muhammad met Adam; in the second heaven, John and Jesus; in the third, Joseph; in the fourth, Idris, about whom God had revealed 'And We exalted him to a place on high!'[21]; in the fifth heaven, he was introduced to Aaron; in the sixth he was

---

[21] Surah 19: 57.

greeted by Moses, and in the seventh he was received by Abraham.

After that the Prophet was taken to paradise, underneath which a river flowed whiter than milk, sweeter than honey. Gabriel told him that this was al-Kaw<u>th</u>ar which God had given to him. Gabriel picked up a handful of earth and lo and behold! it was fragrant musk. Then he was ushered to the Sadratu'l-Muntaha, the Lote-Tree at the end of the Garden. Then His Lord approached him "till He was at a distance of two bows, or even closer" (Q. 53:9). Suddenly the Lote-Tree was covered with a variety of jewels - pearls, rubies, saphires and emeralds.

This was the Prophet's dream. How would you interpret this dream? Some day one of Baháu'lláh's Tablets which He Himself has named Suratu'l Ashab, will be translated and you will read in it such passages as:

> "Say, verily the fragrance of musk has been diffused from the 'Sacred Hills'[22] and the 'Ancient Temples'[23] have been perfumed therefrom. Joy be unto him who is scented by its waft."

Athar-i-Qalam-i-A'la vol. 4, p. 12

"... then mention the Ha (abbreviation for Bahá) at the end of the Names, as spoken by the Holy Dove; perhaps they will be attracted by its melodies. We have mentioned it at the end that people may ascend to the Sadratu'1-Muntaha and seek protection in its shade. Say: By God! The Sadrat has, in truth, overshadowed all that are in the heavens and in the earth. Blessed is he who dwells nigh in its shelters."

Ibid, p.12

---

[22] This metaphoric expression is not clear to the author. This may be a reference to Himself.

[23] This metaphoric expression is not clear to the author. This may be a reference to the former manifestations.

"... Sanctify the mirrors of your souls, O peoples of the earth, then ascend unto the station behind which God has made mention of 'two bows and even closer'."

Ibid p.18

Also, from other Tablets and Prayers:

"Then arose the rustlings of the Sadratu' l-Muntaha in the Abhá Paradise and, calling the denizens of the earth and heaven, said, 'Rejoice and celebrate for the Hand of Bestowal has spread the means of joy in the name of God, the Beauteous, amidst the dwellers of the Tabernacle of Bahá in these splendrous days..."

Ad'iyiyi Mahbub p. 294

"O my God, my Adored One, my Desire! I beseech Thee, in utter contribution and supplication, to protect me from the evil of the clamorous opposer, and to deprive me not of the shelter of the Sadratu' l-Muntaha and the screeching of the Pen of the Most High..."

Ibid, p. 312

"The Sadratu' l-Muntaha is speaking, listen heartily; the Tongue of the God of Mercy is in utterance, be attentive unto it. Thus warneth your Lord, the Speaker, the All-Knowing!"

'Iqtidarat', p. 246

(Above passages are Author's translations)

In scores of other Tablets, Baháu'lláh refers to Himself as the Sadratu' l-Muntaha - the divine Lote-Tree. A few are cited below.

"I have, moreover, with the hand of divine power, unsealed the choice wine of My Revelation, and have wafted its holy, its hidden, and musk-laden fragrance upon all created things."

Gleanings, p. 328

"Whoso hath recognized the Day Spring of Divine guidance and entered His holy court hath drawn nigh unto God and attained His Presence, a Presence which is the real Paradise, and of which the loftiest mansions of heaven are but a symbol. Such a man hath attained the knowledge of the station of Him Who is 'at the distance of two bows,' Who standeth beyond the Sadratu' l-Muntaha."

Gleanings, p. 70

"Advance, O people, with snow-white faces and radiant hearts, unto the blest and crimson spot, wherein the Sadratu' l-Muntaha is calling: 'Verily, there is none other God beside Me, the Omnipotent Protector, the Self-Subsisting!' "

Gleanings, p. 198

"This is the Day wherein the earth hath told out her tidings and hath laid bare her treasures; when the oceans have brought forth their pearls and the divine Lote-Tree its fruit..."

Writings of Bahá'u'lláh, p. 223

"O thou who hast quaffed the wine of My utterance from the chalice of My knowledge! These sublime words were heard today from the rustling of the divine Lote-Tree which the Lord of Names hath, with the hand of celestial power, planted in the all highest Paradise."

Ibid, p. 187

"O kindreds of the earth! Incline your ears unto the Voice from the divine Lote-Tree which overshadoweth the world and be not of the people of tyranny on earth."

Ibid, p. 196

"There hath branched from the Sadratu' l-Muntaha this sacred and glorious Being, this Branch of Holiness ('Abdu' l-Bahá); well is it with him that hath sought His shelter and abideth beneath His shadow."

(Tablet of the Branch), cited in
'The World Order of Bahá'u'lláh', p. 135

OPEN DECLARATION

The first response of the wealthy nobility of the Qurau<u>sh</u> to The Prophet's call was an attitude of indifference. After all, Muhammad had been known as an honest, trustworthy man with unblemished character. He was born into a noble family, one of the noblest of the Qurau<u>sh</u>, fostered by Abu Talib, an elder notable of Makkah. He was the husband of the wealthy, highly respected <u>Kh</u>adija. They were baffled by His claim and astonished at what he said. Some thought he was possessed; others considered his utterances reveries and spun tales of the ancients; still others believed he was trying to be a poet, and there were those who said he was a sorcerer.

ˑBut God's Revelations were intended to guide them from the darkness of ignorance, idol worship, and fruitless and demeaning practices to the light of Truth and the worship of the one God, and to unite the divergent, feuding tribes of the Arabian Peninsula into a vibrant, flourishing nation, and to bring about a transformation and a revival in the decaying bones of the followers of former religions. So Revelations came to Muhammad to break away with the past and to summon his compatriots to the unity of God and the falsehood of associating other gods with Him.

Profess publicly then thou hast been bidden, and
withdraw from those who join gods to God.
Verily, We will maintain thy Cause against those
who deride thee,
Who set up gods with God: and at last shall they
know their folly.

Q. 15: 94-96

and:

Call not thou on any other god but God, lest thou be of
those consigned to torment.
But warn thy relatives of nearer kin.
And kindly lower thy wing over the faithful who
follow thee.
And if they disobey thee, then say, 'Verily, I am clear
of that which ye do;'
And put thy trust in Him that is the Mighty, the
Merciful.

Q. 26: 213-217

Some have reported that the Prophet invited his relatives,
including his uncles Abu Talib, Hamzih, al-'Abbas and Abu
Lahab, some forty men, and ordered 'Alí to prepare a meal
for them. A leg of mutton, a bowl of milk and some wheatmeal
was all he could prepare. The Prophet blessed it and said,
"Take in the name of God." They all ate of it and were filled.
Likewise one bowl of a beverage was brought from which all
drank and were satisfied. But when the repast was over, it
was as though the food and the drink had not been touched.
When Muhammad rose to address the assembled company,
his uncle Abu Lahab got in ahead of him and said, "Your
host has bewitched you." They then broke up before the
Prophet of God could find a chance to address them.

But the invitation was renewed for the following day and
everything proceeded as in the previous day. Then the
Prophet said, 'O sons of 'Abd-al-Muttalib! God has
commanded that I summon you to Him. Surely no Arab has
brought his people a more glorious Message. Who will swear
fealty to me and assist me in this undertaking to become my
brother, my executor and my successor?' All remained silent,
except 'Alí, the youngest, the fattest in body and the thinnest
in legs, who arose and declared: 'O Prophet of God, I will be
your helper in this matter.' Laying his hand on 'Alí's shoulder,
the Prophet said, 'This is my brother, my executor, and my

successor among you. Hearken to him and obey him.' The men got up laughing. One said to Abu Talib, mockingly, "He has ordered you to listen to your son and obey him!"

Others, however, have reported that when the Prophet received God's Revelation to proclaim the Message to his kith and kin, He mounted al-Safa, and called out: "O Sons of 'Abd al-Muttalib; O Sons of 'Abd Manaf; O Sons of Qusayy," and continued naming the Quraysh clan by clan, "I call you to God and warn you of His punishment," Some asked, "Who is that calling out?" "It is Muhammad," others replied. Then they gathered around him. He said to them, "If I were to tell you that horsemen were coming out at the foot of that mountain, would you believe me?" "We have never known you to tell a lie," they answered. Then he said, "I am a warner admonishing you to beware of a terrible doom." His uncle Abu Lahab retorted, "May you perish! Did you assemble us all together for this?" Whereupon God revealed the following Sura:

> The Hands of Abu Lahab shall perish,
> and he shall perish.
> His riches shall not profit him,
> neither that which he hath gained.
> He shall burn in a flaming fire;
> And his wife — the bearer of wood,
> On her neck a cord of twisted fibres of a palm tree.
>
> Q. Sura 111.

The allusions in this Sura are better appreciated when it is understood that Abu Lahab had a hot temper and so was given this nickname which means father of flame. His wife was a wealthy woman proud of a jewelled necklace which she wore. It is said that Abu Lahab went around calling Muhammad his crazy nephew. His wife, too, carried bundles of thorn and scattered them over the Prophet's path by night, and spread slanderous reports about him. Abu Lahab's life ended in great distress. He had not participated in the Battle of Badr, but had arranged with a debtor who owed him 4000 dirhams to go in his stead, foregoing his claim to the debt amount. When so many of the chiefs of Quraysh fell on the battlefield, he was struck with a guilty conscience and fell into deep remorse for his failure to fight by their side. This added to the loss of his son, who was torn to pieces by a lion while travelling to Syria surrounded by the caravan, caused much pain and grief. He was smitten with postules from which he died only a week after the news of the disastrous defeat of the Quraysh at Badr reached Makkah. His sons left the body unburied for three days for fear of catching the disease themselves. The stinking odor became unbearable. Neighbours upbraided the sons for neglecting to pay due respect to their dead father to give him a decent burial. In the end hired black slaves undertook the task. They dug a shallow grave along a wall, dumped the body into it, threw water upon it from a distance and covered it with stones thrown over the wall. Sale comments: "And accordingly his great possessions, and the rank and esteem in which he lived in Mecca, were of no service to him, nor could protect him against the vengeance of God." [24]

It is said that his wife was strangled by the very rope with which she carried the thorns that she spread along the Prophet's path.

---

[24] See Sale, 'The Koran, p. 595 n. 3 - Frederick Warne, London. Ed. Sale quotes al-Baydawi as his source. I.I. and Tabari make no mention of this incident.

OPPOSITION BEGINS

The Prophet proclaimed the Oneness of God publicly and showed the futility, nay the absurdity of idol worship to the Makkans in accordance with God's behests:

When he (Abraham) said to his father, O my father, why dost thou worship that which heareth not, neither seeth, nor profiteth thee at all?

Q. 19: 42

and:

And rehearse unto them the story of Abraham: when he said unto his father and his people, 'What do ye worship?' They answered, 'We worship idols; and we constantly serve them all the day long.' Abraham said, 'Do they hear you, when ye invoke them?' Or do they either profit you or hurt you?' They answered, 'But we found our fathers do the same.' He said, 'What think ye? That which ye worship, and your forefathers worshipped are my enemy; except only the Lord of all creatures; who hath created me and directed me; and who giveth me to eat and to drink, and when I am sick, healeth me; and who will cause me to die, and will afterwards restore me to life; and who, I hope, will forgive my sins on the day of judgment.'

Q. 26: 69-82

And yet again:

Have ye then considered al-Lat[25] and al-'Uzza[26], and Manat[27], the third one besides? ... They are no other

---

[25] Three goddesses each occupying a shrine not far from Makkah at al-Ta'if, Nakhlah, and al-Mushallal.

[26] Ibid.

[27] Ibid.

than empty names, which ye and your fathers have named. God hath sent no authority for them. They follow no other than a vain opinion, and what (their) souls desire: yet hath the guidance come to them from their Lord. Or shall man have what he wishes?

Q. 53: 19-24

When the Quraysh learned that Muhammad publicly made disparaging remarks about their idols and imputed ignorance to their forefathers, they were insulted and wounded. They decided that he and the small band of his followers were their enemies. But they feared taking any direct action against him as he was under the protection of his uncle Abu Talib, and received strong support from Khadija and her family. They began persecuting the believers, especially the lower classes and the slaves. These were interspersed among the clans of Quraysh; each clan could take care of the believers in its own community without fear of reprisal by members of other clans. They attacked and beat the believers, imprisoned them, cut off the supply of provision to them, left them out in the burning sun of Makkah, inflicted all manner of suffering on them to induce them to recant their Faith.

Bilal is a good example. His master would lay him on his back, naked in the sun, and put a heavy stone on his chest, and would say to him, "You will stay here till you die or deny Muhammad and worship al-Lat and al-Uzza." Patiently enduring the pain, Bilal would cry, "One, One!" Testifying to the unity of God. Abu Bakr, observing this monstrous scene one day, rebuked his master for his cruelty. "Have you no fear of God that you treat this poor fellow like this? How long is it to go on?" remonstrated Abu Bakr. "You are the one who corrupted him, so save him from his plight that you see." The cruel master retorted. "I will do so," said Abu Bakr, "I have got a black slave, tougher and stronger than he, who is a heathen. I will exchange him for Bilal." The master agreed and Bilal was given his freedom. He was the seventh slave Abu Bakr had bought and freed.

Many similar instances took place. The Apostle, fearing the loss of believers who might not endure such harsh afflictions, urged as many as could to emigrate to Abyssinia, a neighbouring land ruled by the Negus who was a tolerant, kind and generous king.

The first party of ten or eleven male and four female emigrants were pursued by a party of Qura*sh* when informed of their departure. Upon arriving at the sea, however, they found out that their victims had already boarded ship and left. The emigrants that followed had to observe secrecy. Eighty one believers in all, men, women and children, left for Abyssinia singly and in small groups and were given refuge by that Christian monarch.

OPPOSITION INTENSIFIES

The Prophet's companions used to pray in the glens outside Makkah. On one such occasion, they were attacked by a band of the Makkans who protested against this departure from their customary mode of praying. Exchange of words led to exchange of blows. Sa'd, one of the Muslims, struck his adversary with the jaw-bone of a camel and wounded him. This was the first bloodshed in Islám.

Meanwhile the Prophet continued teaching publicly and gaining followers especially among the youth of Quraysh. The wealthy magnates of each clan were faced with a very unpleasant situation as they saw people within each clan breaking up into opposing camps. They were bitter and had to take stringent measures to stop the growth of what they considered a cancer in their society. They held council together and agreed to send a delegation to Abu Talib, the nominal guardian and protector of the Apostle. Various accounts have been reported as to how these meetings proceeded. They all agree in essentials and differ only in particulars. Here we narrate one such account, taken at random.

After the usual ceremonial salutations, the delegates sat before him and said, "O Abu Talib! We hold you in great esteem and wish no harm to come to you. Your nephew has abused us, has cursed our gods, affronted our religion, ridiculed our customs and mores and censured our forefathers' beliefs. Either you must check him or we ought to be allowed to deal with him as we deem appropriate." With soft, conciliatory words Abu Talib appeased them and sent them away.

This was no solution to their problem, however, as the breach within the clans worsened almost daily by kinsmen joining the Apostle. So the Makkan leadership had a second council which led to a second visit with Abu Talib. This time they declared that they could no longer endure the vilification of their fathers, the defamation of their gods, and outrage against their customs and traditional practices. They demanded immediate action to stop Muhammad's activities, as, otherwise, they would have to fight both of them until one side was destroyed.

Abu Talib was in a quandary. He loathed enmity with his own people, but was loth to abandon the Apostle to them. After their departure, he sent for his nephew, and informed him of the mood of the Quraysh. "Spare me and yourself," he said. "Do not put on me a burden greater than I can bear." "O my uncle!" answered the Prophet, "by God, if they put the sun in my right hand and the moon in my left on condition that I abandoned this course, until God has made it victorious, or I perish therein, I would not abandon it." Then he broke into tears and got up to leave. "Come back, my nephew," Abu Talib called, and when he came back, he said, "Go and say what you please, for by God I will never give you up on any account."

The chieftains, however, were not pacified. They swore that they would put an end to the God that commanded the Apostle to destroy their traditional way of life. They counselled the members of their clans to have firm belief in their own gods. "This is a thing designed," they said, referring to the Prophet's call, "pay no attention to it."

However the matter remained unresolved to the increasing distress and disappointment of the Quraysh. Their leaders went back to Abu Talib, taking with them 'Umara, a strong, handsome youth, son of al-Walid[28], a wealthy notable of Makkah, and an implacable enemy of the Prophet, offering the youth in exchange for Muhammad. "This will be man for man, "they said. "By God, this is a monstrous thing that you

---

[28] It is generally agreed that verses 11-25 of Sura 74 pertain to him.

would put upon me," answered Abu Talib, "would you give me your son that I should feed him for you, and should I give my son that you should kill him? By God, this shall never be."

The men warned him that his refusal to cooperate would lead to grave consequences for which he alone would be responsible as they had dealt him fairly and had given him every chance to resolve an unsavoury situation. Abu Talib retorted, "You have not treated me fairly, by God, but you have agreed to betray me and incite the people against me, so do what you like."

Abu Talib invited the Banu Hashim and Banu al-Muttalib to unite in supporting and protecting the Messenger of God. He was well pleased when, with the exception of his brother Abu Lahab, all complied.

Conflicts brewed between fathers and sons, brothers sisters, husbands and wives and friends within each clan. Several sons of noblemen accepted Islám.

The Quraysh instigated the simple-minded and the rabble in each clan to fall on the believers, humiliate them, insult and beat them and seduce them from their religion. The people, thus agitated, insulted the Prophet openly, called him a liar, a sorcerer, a man possessed, a crafty spinner of old tales.

One day as a few prominent members of Makkah had assembled in the Mosque and were discussing their plight and the anguish caused by Muhammad in severing the ties of kinship, pronouncing their idolatrous practices[29] foolish and insulting their forefathers as 'people who were not warned, and who lived in negligence,'[30] the Prophet approached, kissed the Black Stone, and circumambulated the Ka'bah.

---

[29] A few of these pagan practices are mentioned to show the transformation that took place in Arab societies when Islám finally triumphed. The practice of slaying or burying alive of female children; the practice of sacrificing a son to an idol if the father would have a number of sons; meat and fruits that were for those who served idols but prohibited to females. See Qur'án VI 137-141 and V 103, 104.

[30] See Q. 36:6; 11:109; 2:170; 5:104.

As he passed them by they heaped insults on him. He ignored them at first and kept on walking around the temple. They continued reviling him every time he approached them. At the end of the third round, he stopped and said, "Will you listen to me, O Quraysh? By him who holds my life in his hand I bring you slaughter." It was as though a thunderbolt had struck. They all stood dumbfounded. One rough-spoken fellow said in a soft, kind voice, 'Leave in peace, O Abu' l-Qasim[31], for by God you are not of a violent nature.' The following day, they all assembled at the Mosque again and were recounting the incident of the previous day, when the Apostle arrived. They all jumped and surrounded him. "Are you the one who said so-and-so against our gods and our religion?" they clamoured. The Apostle said, "Yes, I am the one who said that." One of them seized his robe. But before the crowd could inflict bodily harm on him, Abu Bakr intervened and, with tears welling up in his eyes, said: "Would you kill a man for saying Alláh is my Lord?" Then they let go of him, and the Apostle and Abu Bakr departed.

Not long after this incident, one day, when the Prophet was sitting alone in the mosque some distance apart from where the Quraysh had assembled, 'Utba suggested to his peers in the Assembly to go to the Prophet and find some means of reconciliation with him. They agreed it was a good idea. He joined the Prophet and repeated the grievances which the Quraysh had put before Abu Talib earlier, and offered a few suggestions. The Prophet agreed to hear him through. He went on, "If what you want is money, we will make you the richest man in Makkah; If you are after a high position of honour, we will make you our chief with power to make decisions as you please; if you want to be a king, we shall make you one; if you are unable to get rid of this spirit that haunts you, we will find a physician for you and pay all expenses until you are cured and the familiar spirit that has

---

[31] O Father of Qasim. Quasim was the eldest son of Muhammad.
(This follow the Arab custom of calling a man or a woman, father or mother of an offsprimy)

possessed you is driven away. The Apostle listened patiently. God then sent down a Revelation, which later was named, 'The Distinctly Explained', a Sura now the 41st. The Apostle said "Now listen to what I have to say," and recited:

In the name of God, the Compassionate, the Merciful! H.M. A Revelation from the Compassionate, the Merciful! A Book whose verses are distinctly explained, an Arabic Qur'án for men of understanding; bearing good tidings, and warnings. But most of them turn aside, and hearken not. And they say, 'Our hearts are veiled from that to which thou callest us; and there is a deafness in our ears, and a curtain between us and thee. Act (as thou thinkest right). We verily shall act (as we think right)...

The Sura consists of 54 verses. God explains to the Quraysh that He is supreme in might and that He is the creator of the heavens and the earth, and that none can frustrate His purpose. He cites the examples of the tribes of 'Ad and Thamud who at an earlier age showed pride to the Messengers sent to them, ridiculed them and turned aside from God's commands, and how their end was naught but destruction. He promises the believers good tidings in this world and in the world to come, and threatens the unbelieving idolators with punishment of shame in both worlds. He urges the Quraysh to worship God alone, and renounce idolatry; He reasons with them that the worship of idols has degraded them, kept them in ignorance, ruined them and they have become a lost people. "Who speaketh better than he who inviteth unto God, and worketh righteousness, and saith, 'I am a Muslim?' Good and evil shall not be held equal. Turn away evil with that which is better." And in this vein, it continues. The reading of this Sura is highly recommended.

'Utba listened attentively. When the Prophet finished his recitation, he prostrated himself and said, "You have heard what you have heard, Abu' l-Walid; the rest remains with you."

They say that when 'Utba rejoined his companions, his expression had completely changed. When asked what had happened, he said, "I heard words such as I had never heard before; they were neither poetry, nor spells, nor witchcraft. My advice is to leave this man alone. His message will set the tribes ablaze. If they kill him, your purpose is accomplished by other hands than ours; if he gains victory, his power will be our power, his prestige our prestige, his prosperity our prosperity." They all proclaimed, "He has bewitched you with his tongue."

THE CONVERSION OF HAMZIH AND 'UMAR

Hamzih, the Prophet's uncle, who later proved to be a stalwart champion of Islám and whom the Apostle is recorded to have given the appelation "the Lion of God and of His . Apostle,"[32] loved hunting. It was his habit, when returning from a hunt, to visit the Ka'bah and circumambulate it before going home. Returning from one of these hunts, he was accosted by a woman who informed him of what she had witnessed earlier in the day. "While the Apostle was sitting by al-Safa," she reported, "Abu Jahl passed by, insulted and abused him and his religion and grossly humiliated him. The Messenger of God said nothing and Abu Jahl left to attend the assembly of Quraysh at the Ka'bah." Hamzih was furious and set forth towards the Ka'bah, not stopping to greet anyone. He found Abu Jahl sitting among the people. He went up to him, stood over him, and violently struck him a blow with his bow. "Will you insult him when I follow his religion, and say what he says?" he cried, "Hit me back if you can!" Some members of his clan got up to go to Abu Jahl's defence, but he said, "Let Abu 'Umara alone for, by God, I insulted his nephew deeply." Hamzih's confession was a clear indication that he had now accepted Islám, and would follow the Prophet's commands. God then revealed:

> Shall he (Hamzih) who hath been dead, and whom We have restored unto life, and unto whom We have ordained a light (the Qur'án), whereby he may walk among men, be as he (Abu Jahl) whose similitude is in darkness (idolatry) from whence he shall not come forth?

Q. 6: 122

---

[32] Known also by the title, the 'Prince of Martyrs'. Iqán, p. 121.

'Umar's conversion was no less dramatic. 'Umar was a strong, stubborn, passionate man who treated the Apostle's followers harshly and violently. Like Saul of Tarsus, he looked for an excuse to inflict pain on the believers and persecute them. It so happened that his own sister Fatima and her husband Sa'id had accepted Islám, and were ardent followers of the Apostle, but kept the matter concealed from him.

One day 'Umar, girth with his sword, intent upon killing the Apostle and his companions, was walking briskly towards al-Safa, where he had been informed the Prophet and some forty men and women had gathered, when a friend met him and asked where he was going. "I am making for Muhammad, the apostate, who has split up the Quraysh, made mockery of their traditions, insulted their faith and their gods, to kill him." "You deceive yourself, 'Umar," his friend answered. "Do you suppose that the Banu Abd Manaf will allow you to walk upon the earth when you have killed Muhammad? Had not you better go back to your own family and set their affairs in order?" "What is the matter with my family?" 'Umar asked. "Your brother-in-law and your sister Fatima have both become Muslims. You had better go and deal with them."

'Umar then directed his steps towards his sister's house. He reached it when Khabbab was reciting the recently revealed Sura Ta Ha (Sura 20) of the Qur'án. When 'Umar's voice was heard, Khabbab hid himself in an adjoining room, and Fatima hid the manuscript under her thigh. 'Umar, who had heard a voice reading something said, "What was this nonsense I heard?" "You have heard nothing," they said. "By God, I have," he said, "and I have heard that you follow Muhammad in his religion." Anger was fast building up in him. He seized Sa'id by the collar. His wife jumped up to defend her husband. The blow fell on her and wounded her. Defiant, they admitted that they had, indeed, become Muslims, believed in one God and His Apostle, and that he could do what he liked. Seeing blood on his sister's face, 'Umar felt ashamed and calmed down. He asked to see the writing, as he could read. His sister refused to give him the manuscript and told him that he was unclean and that only the purified could touch the holy Revelations from God.[33] 'Umar thereupon washed himself and she gave him the page on which the Sura Ta Ha was written. When he read a part of it, he was filled with admiration. "This is a noble speech." he said. Khabbab, who was listening in the next room, emerged and said, "O 'Umar, by God, I hope that God has singled you out by His Prophet's call, for but last night I heard Him saying, 'O God, strengthen Islám by Abu' l-Hakam[34] or by 'Umar.' Come to God, come to God, O 'Umar." Thereupon 'Umar asked Khabbab to lead him to the Prophet so that he may accept Islám. Khabbab told him that the Prophet was in a house in al-Safa with a few companions.

When 'Umar knocked on the door of the house where the Prophet and his companions had gathered, the man answering the door was reluctant to admit him. He was not sure of 'Umar's real intent as he had his sword on, but the Prophet called that he be admitted, and rose to receive him. He then seized him by his girdle and dragged him forcibly, saying "What has brought you, son of al-Khattab, for by God, I do not think you will cease (your persecution) until God brings calamity upon you."[35] 'Umar replied, "O Apostle of God, I have come to you to confess my belief in God and His Apostle and what He has brought from God." The Messenger of God gave thanks to God with such fervour that all knew 'Umar had become a Muslim.

---

[33] This was based on a previous Revelation: Q. 56:77-79 "Verily, this is an honourable Qur'án. In a Book, Preserved, None toucheth it, but the purified."

[34] Abu'l-Hakam (Father of wisdom) was Abu Jahl's title. The Prophet named him Abu Jahl (Father of Ignorance) because of his stubborn resistance to God's summons.

[35] Compare with Jesus's words to Saul, Acts 9: 4, 5: "... Saul, Saul why persecutest thou me.. , it is hard for thee to kick against the pricks."

The conversion of two stalwart, weighty personalities of the Qura<u>sh</u>, Hamzih and 'Umar, was cause for jubilation.

The companions were sure that the Messenger of God would henceforth be amply protected.

THE FIRST BELIEVER TO RECITE
THE QUR'ÁN PUBLICLY

'Abdullah b. Masud was the son of a slavewoman, and a poor shepherd in Makkah. When a few of the Prophet's companions one day suggested that it would be a good idea if someone recited the Qur'án in a loud, clear voice to the Quraysh in the hope that they would listen to it, 'Abdullah volunteered to do it. At first, they did not think he was a suitable candidate for the job. "Perhaps a person of better breeding would be more appropriate and would have better protection if the people attacked him" they thought. But Abdullah assured them that he was not afraid of the people. "Let me alone. God is my protector," he said.

So one morning he went to the Mosque where the Quraysh usually assembled. He stood at the Maqam[36] and recited in a loud voice: In the name of God, the Compassionate, the Merciful," and, raising his voice, continued, "The Compassionate Who taught the Qur'án." A few people close to him said, "What on earth is this son of a slavewoman saying?" Then it struck them that he was reading the Prophet's Words. They attacked him and hit him, but he continued to read to the end. The believers noticed the effect of the blows upon his face, and said, "This is just what we feared would happen to you." He said, "God's enemies were never more contemptible in my sight than they are now, and

---

[36] 'The Place of Abraham. It is true that a particular place, a small building supported by six pillars about 8 feet high, situated in the Ka'bah, is known by this name, and was so known in the time of the Prophet and even before him...' Maulana Muhammad 'Alí f.n. 1686, p. 55. 'Holy Qur'án.

if you like I will go and do the same thing before them tomorrow." They said, "No, you have done enough, you have made them listen to what they don't want to hear."

This same 'Abdullah discovered Abu Jahl among the corpses lying in the battlefield at Badr a few years later in Medina. He had not died yet. He put his foot on his neck and reminded him of all the evil he had caused, cut off his head and brought it to the Prophet. Later he was put in charge of the treasury of Kufah by the Caliph 'Umar.

PERSECUTION CONTINUES

Filled with despair as it became obvious that Abu Talib would not intervene with Muhammad to curb his activities, the Quray<u>sh</u> resorted to other devices in the hope of accomplishing their purpose. They sent emissaries to Abyssinia to induce the Negus to repatriate the Muslims who had emigrated to that land. However, the Negus was well-pleased with the immigrants, and Ja'far, one of the immigrants and 'Alí's brother, defended the Apostle and his teachings before the Negus in a very eloquent and convincing language, showing how through those teachings they were able to abandon a barbaric way of life and adopt humane manners and worthy habits conducive to a happier and more fulfilling life. So the emissaries' pleas and solicitations were of no avail and they returned empty-handed.

Having failed in this attempt, and seeing the increasing number of converts to Islám, which now included Hamza, the Prophet's uncle, and 'Umar b. al-Khattab, they held another conference to deliberate on the step to take next to stop the tide that was fast engulfing them on all sides.

They decided to sever all social ties with the Banu Hashim and Banu al-Muttalib from whom Muhammad, his uncles and cousins had descended — all except Abu Lahab the uncle who hated Muhammad and his Cause to the end of his life. They agreed not to marry their women nor give women of their own clans to any of them in marriage. They also pledged not to sell or buy anything to and from them. They wrote down their pledges in the form of a binding contract and posted it in the Ka'bah to give the document more solemnity.

This action rather than intimidate the Banu Hashim and Banu al-Muttalib, strengthened the bond of kinship among them. They now joined Abu Talib solemnly pledging to protect the Prophet at all costs.

The boycott continued for over three years. Business slackened and people realized that the measure enforced by their leaders had no advantage and was costly for them. Goods reached the enemy by clandestine means. The story goes that Abu Jahl met a man one day carrying a sack of wheat of <u>Kh</u>adija, the Apostle's wife. He stopped him, took him to task for breaking the boycott and told him that he would disgrace him in Makkah for doing it. A passerby came up and wanted to know what was going on. When he learned the circumstances, he told Abu Jahl that the wheat belonged to <u>Kh</u>adija and was stored in the man's house. "Would you prevent him from taking her own food to her?" and added, "Let him go". Abu Jahl refused to do so and, after an exchange of verbal abuse, they came to blows. The man struck Abu Jahl's head with a camel's jawbone, split it open, pushed him to the ground and trampled upon him. The sack of wheat reached its destination. This and similar incidents made the boycott ineffective.

In the end five judicious members of the various Quray<u>sh</u> clans recognized the absurdity of the boycott, leagued together and decided to have it repealed. One of these, Zuhayr, after the customary circumambulation of the Ka'bah seven times, stood before the people and said, "People of Makkah, shall we eat food, drink, and wear clothes while the Banu Hashim are perishing, neither buying, nor selling? By God, I shall not sit down until this unjust document which severs relationships is torn up." Abu Jahl, sitting in the Mosque, said, "You lie, by God. It shall not be torn up." A man shouted, "By God, you are a greater liar. We did not approve of its being written when it was written." Another said, "He speaks the truth. The document does not have our approval and we do not acknowledge it." Someone else spoke up, saying, "You have both spoken the truth and anyone who differs is lying. We feel guilty before God for what is written in it."

It is said that when a man went to pull the document down, he found that ants had eaten all except the heading, "In your name, O God!"

Meanwhile the Messenger of God continued his teaching work vigilantly despite opposition and obstructions. Nothing seemed to hinder his zeal and effort in obedience to God's command.

INSTANCES OF PERSECUTION

Persecution and opposition took different forms in Makkan society. Some were physical, such as beatings, spitting on faces, subjecting the naked body of a slave to the scorching heat of the Arabian mid-day sun while a heavy stone was put on his chest in the hope of forcing him to recant his faith, as in the case of Bilal, making life in the community so intolerable as to force exodus and take refuge in a foreign land, refusing to transact business with individuals or groups, throwing filthy objects, such as a sheep's uterus upon the Messenger as he was praying, or throwing it in his cooking pot when food was being prepared for him, throwing thorns, thistles and garbage in his path, etc. etc. Some were psychological — jeering, mocking, verbal insults, fake accusations, reviling, engaging in senseless, childish disputes and argumentation — any act that would humiliate the Messenger of God and his followers. But, I believe the hardest affliction for the Prophet was that he had to suffer the ignorance of the Quraysh and their resistance to and denial of the truth. Here was a kind, compassionate soul who was convinced himself to be the bearer of His Word, and a beacon beaming the light of truth. To him Revelations were the irrefutable commands of God. He was saddened and suffered fits of depression when he encountered stubborn and irrational opposition from the wealthy dignitaries of Makkah who doubted his divine Mission, showed total lack of understanding of his teachings, and were adamant to follow the beliefs of their forefathers. God revealed concerning them:

> But they say, 'Verily we found our fathers with a faith, and verily, in their footsteps we follow.' And likewise 'We sent not, before thy time, a warner to any city but its wealthy ones said, "Verily we found our fathers with a faith, and verily, in their footsteps we are guided."

Say, "What! even though I bring you a better guidance than that you found your fathers following?" They said "Verily, we believe not in that with which you have been sent." Wherefore we took vengeance on them, and behold what hath been the end of those who accused our Messengers of imposture.'

Q. 43: 22-25

Al-Walid was a very wealthy man in Makkah and an inveterate enemy of the Messenger of God. It is reported that he once said, 'Does God send down revelations to Muhammad and ignore me, the greatest chief of Quraysh, to say nothing of Abu Masud, the chief of Thaqif, we being the great ones of Ta'if and Makkah?' God sent the following Revelation concerning him, but the lesson is good for all humanity for all time:

And now that the truth is come unto them, they say, 'This is a piece of sorcery: and we believe not therein.' And they say, 'Had but this Qur'án been sent down unto some great man of either of the two cities...!' Do they distribute the mercy of thy Lord![37] We distribute their necessary provision among them, in this present life, and we raise some of them degrees above the others, that the one of them may take the other to serve him: and the mercy of thy Lord is more valuable than the riches they hoard. But for fear that all mankind would have become a single people of unbelievers, verily we would certainly have given to those who believe not in the God of Mercy roofs of silver to their houses, and silver stairs to ascend by; and doors of silver to their houses, and couches of silver to recline on; and ornaments of gold; for all these are merely the good things of the present life; but the next life doth thy Lord reserve for those who fear Him. And whoso shall withdraw from the remembrance of the Merciful, we

---

[37] i.e. the Messenger of God is His mercy and gift to mankind.

will chain a Satan unto him, and he shall be his fast
companion.

Q. 43: 30-37

Ubayy and 'Uqbah, two bosom friends, vehemently
opposed the Messenger of God. On one occasion, 'Uqbah
had sat with the Apostle and listened to his discourse. This
made Ubayy very angry. He vowed never to associate with
'Uqbah again unless he would spit in the Prophet's face and
stop meeting him. Rather than lose a close friend, 'Uqbah
actually did that. Some say God revealed these verses
concerning them, but they are truths that have universal
application:

And on the day when the wrongdoer will bite his hands,
saying: 'Oh! Would that I had taken the same Path
with the Messenger! Oh! Woe is me! Would that I had
not taken on one for a friend! It was he who led me
astray from the Warning which had reached me! And
Satan has ever been for man a failure.

Q. 25: 27-29

'Uqbah was one of the captives of the Battle of Badr and
was killed by the Apostle's order.

One day, as the Apostle of God was circumambulating
the Ka'bah, three notables of Makkah, his uncompromising
enemies, called him to meet with them. They suggested that
Muhammad and the Quraysh would unite in the worship of
his God and their deities at the same time so they would all
benefit and end their conflict; they would worship the God of
Muhammad one year on condition that Muhammad would
worship their gods the following year and continue in this
manner alternately every year. God then sent down the
following Revelation:

Say: O ye unbelievers! I worship not that which ye
worship, and ye do not worship that which I worship; I
shall never worship that which ye worship, neither will

ye worship that which I worship. To you be your religion;
to me my religion.

Q. 109: 1-6

As everyone knows, God is not a respecter of
personalities[38]. Rank, wealth, colour and sex each play an
important role in this contingent world, but God rewards
persons for their faith, purity of heart and motive and
excellence of deeds. Whenever the Apostle sat in the mosque
with ordinary believers, the Quraysh said mockingly to one
another, "These are his associates, as you see. Muhammad's
claim is, no doubt, a lie. God never could choose these and
prefer them to us." They pretended to be willing to accept
the Prophet, if the poor and the lower classes were sent away
from his company. God then revealed concerning them:

> Drive not away those who call upon their Lord morning
> and evening, desiring (to behold) His face. Thou art
> not accountable for them in aught; nor are they
> accountable for thee in aught that thou shouldst drive
> them away and that thou become one of the unjust.
> Thus have We proved some of them by others, that
> they may say, "Are these (the people) among us unto
> whom God hath been gracious?" Doth not God best
> know the grateful? And when they who believe in Our
> signs shall come unto thee, say, "Peace be upon you.
> Your Lord hath prescribed unto Himself mercy; so that
> whoever among you worketh evil through ignorance,
> and afterwards repenteth and amendeth, then He surely
> is the Gracious, the Merciful."

Q. 6: 52-54

The Apostle, it is said, often sat with a young Christian
slave, named Jabr. According to Noldeke, he must have been
an Abyssinian slave boy, named Gebru, meaning 'slave of'
in Ethiopian; others say, he was a Greek servant who could

---

[38] See Rom 2:11; Eph. 6:9; Col. 3:25; Jas. 2:1-7.

read and write well. The Quraysh believed that Muhammad learned most of what he said from this Christian slave of Banu al-Hadrami. God revealed the following concerning this:

> We also know that they say, "Verily, a certain man teacheth him to compose the Qur'án. The tongue of the person unto whom they incline, is a foreign tongue, while this Qur'án is in plain Arabic.

Q. 16: 103[39]

The indignities that the Messenger of God endured patiently are too numerous to be recounted here. His patience emboldened his adversaries who stopped at nothing to revile and deride and persecute him. Even as he was engaged in prayer, they pelted him with stones and threw filthy objects at him. Tabari says, 'Finally, I have been told, he took a large stone and sheltered behind it when he prayed.' But nothing deterred him from teaching the Oneness of God to a perverted, misguided people, day and night. His faith in God, the source of Truth never wavered.

---

[39] For further elaboration on this subject, see the 'Koran', Sales translation, f.n.2.

THE SO-CALLED SATANIC VERSES

To indulge in lurid tales and fanciful stories is not proper for the seeker of truth. However, it is fitting that the reader becomes acquainted with what has assumed sensational reporting in recent times. And for this reason alone I venture to lay the facts before the reader.

The incident, as related by Tabari[40] , and, as far as I know, by only one earlier chronicler, al-Waqidi, is based on two reports:

1. Ibn Humayd - Salama - Muhammad b. Ishaq - Yazid b. Ziyad al-Madani - Muhammad b. Ka'b al-Qurazi[41]. The sequence of events is summarized as follows:

a) The Messenger of God grieved because the Quraysh rejected the message of God. He longed for a sign from God that would be a means of reconciliation with them for their own welfare.

b) God revealed the Sura known 'the Star' (Sura 53): "By the Star when it setteth, your companion[42] erreth not, nor is he led astray: neither doth he speak of his own will."

And when the two verses, 19 and 20 were uttered:

"What think ye of Allat, and Al'Uzzah, and Manat[43] the other, the third?"

---

[40] The History of al-Tabari, vol. 6, # 1192-1196, pp. 107-112.

[41] "He was from the Banu Qurayzah (one of the three Jewish tribes resident at Madinah). It was probably his father or grandfather who was converted to Islám. He died in A.H. 108-120, AD 726-738," (cited in the History of al-Tabari, vol. 9, p. 56, footnote 390).

[42] Referring to the Apostle who was charged with falsehood and being possessed.

[43] Names of three godesses. Their shrines were located not far from Makkah at al-Ta'if, Nakhla, and al-Mushallal, respectively. (Cited in the History of al-Tabari, Vol. 6, translator's forward, p. 42).

"Satan cast on his tongue, because of his inner debates and what he desired to bring to his people, the words:

"These are high-flying cranes; verily their intercession, is accepted with approval."[44]

c) The Quraysh were elated at the manner in which Muhammad spoke of their godesses. The believers accepted it as true Revelation and did not suspect him of error, illusion, or mistake.

d) The Revelation continued uninterruptedly to the end of the Sura. Muhammad prostrated, as bidden in the last verse, and so did the believers and the Quraysh polytheists who were present in the mosque.

e) "The news of this prostration reached those of the Messengers of God's Companions who were in Abyssinia and people said, 'The Quraysh have accepted Islám'. Some rose up to return, while others remained behind..."

f) "Then Gabriel came to the Messenger of God and said, 'Muhammad, what have you done? You have recited to the people that which I did not bring to you from God, and you have said that which was not said to you!"

g) "Then the Messenger of God was much grieved and feared God greatly."

h) But God was merciful to him and consoled him with this Revelation (Q. 22: 52)

"We have sent no apostle, or prophet, before thee, but, when he read, Satan suggested some error in his reading. But God shall make void that which satan hath suggested: then shall God confirm His signs; for God is knowing and wise."

---

[44] An alternative reading would render it 'is to be desired or hoped for' (ibid, p. 108, footnote 172).

i) "Thus God removed the sorrow from His Messenger, reassured him about that which he had feared and cancelled the words which Satan had cast on his tongue..."

j) The new Revelations (vs. 21-26) now read:

"Have ye male children, and God female? This, therefore is an unjust partition to the words: unto whom He shall please and shall accept."

2. The second report reads:

Al-Qasim b. al-Hasan - al-Husayn b. Daud-Hajja Abu Ma'shar-Muhammad b. ka'b al-Qurazi and Muhammad b. Qays: The events narrated in this report are similar to the first, with a few exceptions:

a) "The Messenger of God was sitting in a large gathering of Quray<u>sh</u>, wishing that day that no revelation would come to him from God which would cause them to turn away from him. Then God revealed..."

b) After the prostration at the end of the Sura, the Quray<u>sh</u> showed their satisfaction in these words: "We recognize that it is God Who gives life and death, Who creates and Who provides sustenance, but if these gods of ours intercede for us with Him, and if you give them a share, we are with you."

c) "That evening Gabriel came to him and reviewed the Sura with him, and when he reached the two phrases which Satan had cast upon his tongue he said, 'I did not bring you these two.' Then the Messenger of God said, 'I have fabricated things against God and have imputed to Him words which He has not spoken'.

Then God revealed to him: (Q. 17: 73-75)

"It wanted little but (the unbelievers) had tempted thee to swerve from (the instructions) which We had revealed unto thee, that thou shouldest devise concerning Us a different thing.

to the words :

> And thou shouldest not have found any to protect thee against Us.

He remained grief-stricken and anxious until the Revelation of the verse: (22:52)

> "We have sent no apostle or prophet, before thee, but when he read, Satan suggested some error in his reading.

to the words :

> for God is Knowing and Wise!"

In this second narration, Gabriel comes to the Prophet that very evening while the return of a body of the believers from Abyssinia occurs later. Gabriel is also specific that Satan interjected only two phrases in Muhammad's tongue and said, "I did not bring you these two." These must have logically been verses 21 and 22. Furthermore verses 73-75 of Sura 17 are introduced as a Revelation to console Muhammad. But he remains grief-stricken until the Revelation of Sura 22 of which verse 52, finally removes the Apostle's grief.

So much for a summary of the two reports, their contradictions and incoherence.

Analysis of the Reports

Let us now carefully examine the contents of these stories. The first thing that strikes one is that both reports originate from one person, Muhammad b. Ka'b al-qurazi. This Hadith has not been reported in the Sahih of Bukhari, universally acknowledged the most reliable source of Hadith; neither has it been mentioned in the other five compilations of Hadith, altogether known as the Six Accurate Hadith compilations. One wonders whence the story originated. Ibn Ishaq, whose name appears in the chain of reporters by Tabari, is silent about the incident in Ibn Hisham's 'Sirah' extant. Possibly he had recourse to other manuscript copies now lost. Did the story originate from al-Qurazi's father or grandfather? If so, were they the only persons who had first-hand knowledge of the incident?

The second confusing element in the narrative is this: exactly what were the Satanic verses? Assuming verses 21 and 22 to be Satan's interjection, and the Revelation of the Sura to have continued forthwith to the end, as both narratives suggest, followed by prostration, how can one account for verses 23 to 26 which declare unmistakably that the godesses are 'empty names' named by you and your fathers; that they are 'vain opinions' desired by your souls; that no authorization has come from God concerning them; and that the intercession of even the angels of heaven is dependant upon God's permission and acceptance? Or, are we to assume that the Satanic verses included verses 21-26, in which case why do the reporters specifically mention two verses and quote "These are exalted females whose intercession is to be sought?" But even if we consider that the Apostle continued the Sura from verse 27 and continued to the end, we note no indication of a conciliatory attitude towards the polytheists. The Revelation still maintains the central theme of Islám, namely, the Oneness of God, His mercy and justice, and His all-encompassing sovereignty (vs. 31), and condemns the scoffing, the contemptuous and derisive attitude of the Quraysh nobles towards Revelations (vs. 59-62), ending, 'But rather worship God and serve Him'.

The third disturbing factor in the first report relates to the sequence of events. It states that the Emigrants to Abyssinia were informed of what had happened and returned to Makkah assured of the Quraysh's conversion to Islám. "Then Gabriel came to the Messenger of God and said, 'Muhammad, what have you done? You have recited to the people that which I did not bring to you from God...' With the slow means of travel at that time, it must have taken weeks before the

Emigrants would come to know of such a happening and make preparations for the return journey to Makkah. Did that part of the Sura 53 remain uncorrected for all that time? This error in chronology is corrected in the second version.

The fourth inexplicable flaw has to do with the verses quoted in Suras 17 and 22 that, the narrators claim, were revealed to console the Messenger of God. Let us examine them now.

Sura 17: 73-75 reads:

"It wanted little but (the unbelievers) had tempted thee to swerve from (the instructions) which We had revealed unto thee, that thou shouldest devise concerning Us a different thing; and then would they have taken thee for their friend; and unless We had confirmed thee, thou hadst certainly been very near inclining unto them a little. Then would We surely have caused thee to taste the punishment of life, and the punishment of death, and thou shouldest not have found any to protect thee against Us."

Now do these verses expressly state, nay, even slightly imply, that the Prophet had swerved from God's Revelation? God chearly declares that but for His confirming his Messenger's heart, he had certainly been very near inclining unto them a little. Had Muhammad swerved, God says that He would surely have caused him to taste the punishment of death in this world and in the next. Both these declarations testify to Muhammad's innocence of wrongdoing.

Commentators have expressed opinions regarding the occasion of the Revelation of these verses. (Study Sale, footnotes 4 and 5, p. 279).

Sura 22: 51-55 reads:

"But those who strive to invalidate Our signs, shall be inmates of Hell. We have sent no apostle or prophet, before thee, but, when he read, Satan suggested some error in his reading. But God shall make void that which Satan hath suggested: then shall God confirm His signs; for God is knowing and wise. (But this He permitteth), that He may make that which Satan hath suggested, a temptation unto those in whose hearts there is an infirmity, and whose hearts are hardened: (for the ungodly are certainly in a wide disagreement from the truth:) and that they on whom knowledge hath been bestowed may know that this Book is the truth from thy Lord, and may believe therein; and that their hearts may acquiesce in the same: for God is surely the director of those who believe, into the right way. But the infidels will not cease to doubt concerning it, until the Hour of Judgment cometh suddenly upon them; or until the punishment of a grievous Day overtake them."

This Sura was revealed several years after Sura 53.[45]

The consensus of opinion is that the Sura 53 was revealed in the fifth year of Muhammad's call, while part of Sura 22 was revealed just before the Hijrah and part immediately after it. Hence its inclusion by some in the Makkah and by others in the Madinah Suras. Now the traditionalists who hold that God revealed these verses to console His Messenger six or seven years after his alleged error in reproducing His Revelation have gone far astray. Did the Prophet remain grief-stricken for all that time anxiously awaiting receipt of words of consolation form his Lord? That would, indeed, be small comfort!

Verse 51 clearly shows that the admonition is addressed to those who strive to invalidate God's Revelations.

The verses themselves, if examined carefully, express a general statement of truth that in all Dispensations there are those who doubt the wisdom of the Messenger, criticise his

---

[45] See Rodwell, p. 453, footnote 1; Sale, p. 326, footnote 5.

teachings and suggest opinions they consider superior. God voids such satanic suggestions and confirms His laws. This is a test for the unbeliever and the hypocrite, 'those in whose hearts there is an infirmity, and whose hearts are hardened.' It also strengthens the faith of the believer that 'they may believe therein; and that their hearts may acquiesce in the same.'[46] The verse:

> "and they on whom knowledge hath been bestowed may know that this Book (the Qur'án) is the truth from thy Lord, and may believe therein, and that their hearts may acquiesce in the same,"

refutes the least suggestion of error on Muhammad's part in reproducing God's Revelation. If such a misdeed had been committed, who would recognize the Book as the embodiment of truth? Who would believe therein? Whose heart would acquiesce in its contents?

A further testimony to this was revealed by God Verse 31 of Sura 74, considered to be the first revealed after the 'Fatrat' and hence an early Makkan Sura:

> "... that they to whom the Scriptures have been given (Jews and Christians), may be certain of the veracity of this Book, and the true believers may increase in faith; and that those to whom the Scriptures have been given, and the true believers, may not doubt; and that those in whose hearts there is an infirmity, and the unbelievers, may say, 'What mystery doth God intend by this?' "

Had not God revealed in Sura 69: 44-51, a Sura which antedates Sura 53 to silence those who accused His Messenger of falsehood?

---

[46] See Sale, p. 332, footnote 3. Note that after citing the occasion of the revelation of the passage, he states on p. 333: "We are told however by al-Beidawi that the more intelligent and accurate persons reject the aforesaid story."

"If Muhammad had forged any part of these discourses concerning Us, verily We had taken him by the right hand, and had cut in sunder the vein of his heart: neither would We have withheld any of you from chastising him. And verily this Book (the Qur'án) is an admonition unto the pious; and We well know that there are some of you who charge the same with imposture: but it shall surely be an occasion of grievous sighing unto the infidels; for it is the truth of a certainty."

After such a clear warning pronounced by God to the infidels for charging Muhammad with imposture, how can one ascribe deception or even impropriety of any kind to Muhammad? He who harbours such thoughts surely has Satan casting doubts in his mind and heart. He ought to strive to repel the thought by flying for refuge unto the Lord of the Daybreak ... and seek deliverance from the mischief of the whisperer who whispereth evil suggestions into the breasts of men.[47]

God has also testified that the Qur'án is flawless, free from contradictions and defects: Q 18: 1 and 39:28.

"Praise be to God, Who hath sent down unto His servant the Book, and hath not inserted therein any crookedness..."

"An Arabic Qur'án, wherein there is no crookedness."

Thus far we have dealt with the narratives, their discrepencies and incoherence. There are, however, other factors worthy of consideration. One is that Muhammad was beyond reproach in reporting Revelations verbatim even where he himself was reproached by God as an example to the believers. Instances of this are many in the Qur'án.

One such instance is the story of Ibn Umm Maktum, a blind man and a believer who came to the Apostle, while he was teaching the principles of Islám to a wealthy Makkan

---

[47] Q. Suras 113, 114.

chief, al-Walid b. Mughirah, interrupting him and insisting to get answers to his questions. The Prophet ignored him. God revealed concerning this matter:

> He (the Prophet) frowned, and turned aside, because the blind man came unto him: and how dost thou know whether he shall peradventure be cleansed, or be admonished, and the admonition shall profit him? As to him who is wealthy (al-Walid) — to him thou wast all attention. And no blame is on thee, if he purify himself not (i.e. if he does not become a Muslim); but he who cometh to thee earnestly, seeking, and fearing (God), dost thou neglect. Nay! but it (the Qur'án) is a warning; and whoso is willing beareth it in mind.
>
> Q. 80: 1-12

Or:

The Prophet's marriage to Zaynab after she was divorced by Záyd, the Prophet's freedman and adopted son, is reported as Revelations from God (Q. 33: 37-40) and the purpose of the marriage is clearly stated:

> ... We gave her to thee as a wife, so that there should be no difficulty for the believers about the wives of their adopted sons, when they have dissolved their marriage tie...
>
> Q. 33: 37

Here the Prophet himself was made an example for posterity that the prohibition in the Qur'án of marriages of daughters-in-law (4: 23) specifying clearly 'sons who are of your own loins' applied to the wives of natural sons only, as reiterated in verse 5 of Sura 33, the 'Confederates'.

Or:

The Revelation in Sura 66: 1, to wit:

O Prophet! Why dost thou forbid (to thyself) what God

hath made lawful to thee, desiring to please thy wives?
And God is Forgiving, Merciful.

Q. 66: 1

Many yarns have been spun by friend and foe concerning the true circumstances occasioning this last mentioned Revelation. We are not concerned with them here. Our purpose is to reveal the scrupulous honesty of the Prophet in meticulously reporting every word revealed to him by God.

How can one believe that the Prophet omitted this line from the Sura after he had recited it to a large assembly as Revelation? How can one accept that the Messenger of God suffered a 'lapse' or 'fell asleep', or that, in his anxiety to compromise with the polytheists of the Quraysh, had a slip of the tongue and recited the 'Satanic Verses'? Did he not fear God's admonition that He would 'cut in sunder the vein of his heart' and would not withhold others from chastising him?

Another is what God Himself affirms in the first few verses of the very Sura allegedly containing the Satanic Verses by which Muhammad's enemies accuse him of falsehood, and fabricate the story of the 'Satanic Verses'.

By the star when it setteth; your companion (Muhammad) erreth not, nor is he led astray: neither doth he speak of his own will. It is no other than a revelation, which hath been revealed unto him. One mighty in power, endued with understanding, taught it him ...

Q. 53: 1-6

After such a clear testimony from God, the least consideration of Satan's ability to interrupt God's Revelation to His Messenger would be tantamount to disbelief in God's might and sovereignty, even if one believes in the existence of Satan as a personality.

And for Bahá'ís a consideration weightier than all aforementioned arguments, is the confirmation in the Kitáb-i-Aqdas by Bahá'u'lláh that the Messenger of God is the quintessence of innocence and the embodiment of absolute truth. He has no peer in the Supreme Infallibility. Those, therefore, who believe that Muhammad was God's Messenger cannot but believe in His supreme Infallibility and can entertain no doubt that not only the 'Satanic Verses' but any ascription of falsehood to Him has been due to bigotry, prejudice and malice.

A GROUP OF CHRISTIANS
ACCEPT ISLAM

A group of some twenty Christians arrived at Makkah with the purpose of investigating the truth of Islám. Some say they came from Abyssinia; Others maintain they were Christians from Najran.[48] The Apostle sat with them in the mosque and explained his mission to them. When the Qur'án was recited to them, their eyes filled with tears. They recognized Muhammad's claim which corroborated their own Scriptures. When they got up to leave, Abu Jahl and a few others of the Quraysh stopped them. "Your behaviour," they told them, "is most contemptible. You were sent here by your people to gather information for them. Instead, you gave up your own religion and believe in the impostor. How foolish and stupid can you be?" "Peace be with you," they replied, "We will not engage in foolish controversy with you. We have our religion and you have yours. We have not been remiss in seeking what is best."

Some believe that parts of the 28th and the 5th Suras of the Qur'án refer to this incident. Others have reported that they have been revealed concerning the Negus of Abyssinia and his advisors.

And now have We caused Our Word to come unto them, that they may be admonished. They unto whom We have given the Scriptures before It[49], believe in it; and when it is read unto them, say, "We believe therein; it is certainly the truth from our Lord: verily we were

---

[48] A city north-east of San a (al Yaman) and south-east of Ta'if that was ihabited by a Christian tribe.

[49] The Qur'án.

Muslims[50] before this." These shall receive their reward twice because they have persevered, and repel evil by good, and distribute (alms) out of that which We have bestowed on them; and when they hear vain discourse, avoid the same, saying, "We have our works, and ye have your works: peace be on you; we covet not the acquaintance of the ignorant."

Q. 28: 51-55

And when they hear that which hath been sent down to the Apostle, thou shalt see their eyes overflow with tears, because of the truth which they perceive, saying, O Lord! We believe; write us down therefore with those who bear witness (to the truth) ...

Q. 5: 83

---

[50] Muslim means: one who submits to the Will of God.

THE REVELATION OF THE SURA
AL-KAWTHAR

Muhammad's sons did not survive long after their birth. His enemies attributed this to God's displeasure with him and taunted him for being without male offspring. al-'As, an implacable enemy of the Messenger of God, said one day to a few of his peers, "Let him alone. He is childless[51]! He shall not be remembered after he dies, and the matter will rest."

> God revealed respecting this remark:
> Verily We have given thee al-Kawthar[52].
> Pray therefore to thy Lord, and sacrifice.
> Verily he who hateth thee shall be childless.

Q. Sura 108

Many interpretations and Hadith have been reported concerning this Sura. Some say that God has given His Messenger an abundance of blessings, such as wisdom, the Qur'án, intercession and Prophecy. He has also stressed prayer and sacrifice as two great divine teachings. Others say it is a river in Paraside wherein the Apostle is promised to be rewarded with abundant good. They describe the river as being "sweeter than honey, whiter than milk, cooler than snow, and smoother than cream; its banks are of chrysolites, and the vessels to drink thereout of silver; and those who drink of it shall never thirst."

Some early believers have reported that when the Apostle was asked what Kawthar meant, they heard him say, "It is a

---

[51] Khadija bore the Apostle seven children, four daughters: Zaynah, Ruqayyah, Umm Kulthum, Fatimah, and three sons: al-Qasim, al-Tahir, and al-Tayyib. Fatima alone survived him.

[52] From root word 'Kathara', means abundance; it is also used allegorically as a river in Paradise.

river as broad as from San'a' to Ayla. Its water pots are in number as the stars of heaven. Birds go down to it with necks like camels." 'Umar b. al-Khattab said, "O Apostle of God the birds must be happy!" He answered, "He who eats them will be happier still!" He was also heard to have said, "He that drinketh thereof shall never thirst."

Now, we know that water, rain, river, etc. have been used allegorically in all the scriptures to signify the Word of God. As water is absolutely essential for the growth of plants, animals and human beings, and as it washes away bodily impurities, the Word of God is equally essential for the spiritual growth of mankind and for the purification of heart and mind. Without it, the soul withers, morals deteriorate, civilizations decay and perish. Hence the use of water for the Word of God, His Teachings and His Laws[53].

Many are the passages in which Baháu'lláh mentions 'the water of life'. Here is one in His prayers:

I was as one dead, Thou didst quicken me with the water of life. I was withered, Thou didst revive me with the heavenly stream[54] of Thine utterance which hath flowed forth from the Pen of the All-Merciful.

Bahá'í Prayers (U.S.A.) p. 20

The Báb wrote a commentary on this Sura at the time when Sayyid Yahya Darabi had his third audience in His presence. You know, of course, that he was an eminent divine, much respected by the king who sent him to investigate the claim of the Báb, verify or reject its truth and report back to him for appropriate decision. The reader is strongly urged to read this most absorbing account in the 'Dawn-breakers' pages 172 et. seq.

---

[53] See Isa 12:3; 55: 10,11; John 4:10-14; 7:37-39; Q. 50:9-11; 21:30.
[54] The original Persian text is 'from the Kawthar of thine utterance'.

'Abdu'l-Bahá, addressing a believer who had asked him for the meaning of Kawthar, wrote:

"Kawthar is a derivative of the root word 'Kithrat' and means abundance. The divine Kawthar today are the holy breaths that bestow life to spirits[55]." Jesus said: "It is the spirit that quickeneth; the flesh profiteth nothing: the Words that I speak unto you, they are spirit, and they are life."

St. John 6:63

---

[55] Ma'idi-i-Asmani vol. 2, p. 95. Author's translation.

THE DEATH OF KHADIJA AND ABU TALIB

Three years before the Hijra (A.D. 619), both these stalwart defenders of the Apostle died, Khadija was the first believer in Islám; Abu Talib remained unwilling to forgo the religion of his forefathers to the end, although, as long as he lived, he vigorously defended his nephew against the vicious attacks of the Quraysh nobility.

It is said that when Abu Talib fell ill, the Quraysh thought they would make a last attempt to bring about a compromise with the Apostle of God. A body of their chieftains from various clans including 'Utba and Shayba, Abu Jahl, Umayyah and Abu Sufyan went to him pleading their case: "Call your nephew and let us come to terms with him. Let him leave us alone; and we shall leave him alone; let him have his religion and we will have ours." When the Apostle came, Abu Talib said, "Nephew, these notables have come seeking a compromise with you." "Yes," He replied, "they should declare the oneness of God by which they shall be able to rule the Arabs and gain dominion over the Persians." They clapped their hands and said, "Do you want to join all the gods into one God, Muhammad? That would, indeed, be phenomenal! We have not heard of this in the last religion." (meaning Christians because they believe in the Holy trinity). "This fellow is not going to give us anything we want," they said to each other, "so let's go and continue with the religion of our fathers until God judge between us." Then they went away.

God revealed concerning them:

Said. By the Qur'án full of the Remembrance (of God). Verily, the unbelievers are proud and contentious. How many generations have We destroyed before them!

And they cried (for mercy), but there was no longer time to escape. They wonder that a warner from among themselves hath come unto them. And the unbelievers said, "This is a sorcerer, a liar: doth he make the gods one God? Surely this is a strange thing." And the chief men among them departed. "Go, and cleave steadfastly to your gods: verily this is the thing which is designed. We have not heard of this in the last religion. It is but an imposture."

Q. 38: 1-7

and later:

They are certainly infidels, who say, 'God is the third of three: for there is no God besides one God ...

Q. 5: 73

and:

Believe therefore in God, and His Apostles, and say not, 'there are three Gods', forbear this; it will be better for you. God is but one God. Far be it from Him that He should have a son.

Q. 4: 71

MIRACLES NO PROOF OF THE TRUTH OF PROPHETHOOD

The story goes that a famous sorcerer of the Banu 'Amir asked the Messenger of God to show him the seal which was between His shoulders, and promised to cure him if He were under a spell.

The Messenger of God told him, "Do you want me to show you a sign?"

"Yes," the enchanter said, "command that bunch of dates to come to you."

The Prophet looked up, saw the cluster hanging from the date palm and beckoned it. The cluster fell and stood before Him. Baffled, the magician said, "Now order it to return to its original place on the tree." The Prophet ordered it to go back and it did so. The man later related the incident to his clansmen, adding, "O Banu 'Amir, never in my whole life have I seen a greater magician than I saw today."

Now read this story:

Among the Quraysh, none was more powerful than Rukana. One day the Prophet encountered Rukana in one of the mountain passes of Makkah, alone. He asked him why he did not fear God and accept His Messenger. Rukana said that he was not sure that he (Muhammad) was God's true Messenger. "Would you believe I say the truth if we wrestle and I throw you down?" asked the Prophet. He readily agreed. They wrestled and Muhammad threw him to the ground easily. Nonplussed, Rukana said, "Do it again, if you can, Muhammad." And He did it the second time. "This is amazing, " Rukana said, "can you really throw me?" "I can do more wonderful things," said the Apostle. "Do you see that yonder tree? I can call it to come to me." "Call it," he asked. He called and the tree advanced and stood before him. Then he ordered it to go back and it returned to its original place.

Rukana went to his kinsfolk and told them what had happened between him and the Prophet, and that he had never seen such sorcery in his life.

Of course, we realize that the Prophet perhaps never indulged in any such miraculous feats, not because he was not able to do so with God's permission, but because such actions did not prove that he was a true Messenger of God, as evident from the impression they left on the people who apparently witnessed their performance. Both the sorcerer of the Banu 'Amir tribe and Rukana, the giant wrestler, ascribed the Prophet's marvellous deeds to sorcery. We are told in the Qur'án that God refused to gratify the people's desire to see Muhammad perform miracles, and reminded them that His Book and His Words were sufficient guidance, and the Balance with which man would be judged.

"Nothing hindered Us from sending miracles, except that the former nations charged them with imposture."

Q. 17: 59

"... And it was not for any Messenger to bring a sign, save by God's permission; so when God's command comes, judgment is given with truth, and those who treat it as a lie are lost."

Q. 40: 78

"They say, 'Unless a sign be sent down unto him from his Lord' (we will not believe). Say: 'Signs are in the power of God alone, and I am only a plain warner.' Is it not enough for them that We have sent down unto thee the Book to be recited to them? Verily, herein is a mercy,.

and an admonition unto people who believe."

Q. 29: 50, 51

"Though We opened to them a gate in heaven and they kept on ascending thereto, they would surely say, 'Our eyes have been dazzled; nay, we are a people bewitched.' "

Q. 15: 14, 15

There are more verses in the Qur'án relating to this matter, but the aforementioned should be sufficient to prove the inefficacy of miracles as proof of the truth of a Messenger of God.

THE APOSTLE GOES TO AL TA'IF TO CONVEY GOD'S MESSAGE TO THAQIF

About sixty miles south-east of Makkah, lies the town of Ta'if. At the time of Muhammad, this was the third most important town of Hijaz, after Makka and Yathrib. Located in an altitude of about 6000 feet above sea-level, it boasts the most salubrious climate in the Peninsula, where, it is reported, that water freezes in certain years, and the most luxuriant vegetation of all kinds — figs, grapes, melons, peaches, almonds and pomegranates — are produced. It was, and still is, the summer resort of the Makkan aristocracy.

To this town, Muhammad now directed his steps to teach the Faith of God to the tribe of Thaqif and their chiefs. He met three brothers, 'abd Yalayl, Mas'ud, and Habib, then chiefs of the tribe. When he gave them the Message and invited them to support Islám, they ridiculed him. One of them said, "If God has sent you, I will tear off the covering of the Ka'bah." The other said, "Could God find no man better than you to send?" The third said, "By God, don't let me speak to you, ever. If you are an apostle from God, as you say you are, I am far too insignificant to reply to you, and if you are lying against God, it is not right that I should talk with you!" So the Apostle left them.

The chiefs then instigated the rabble to insult him, jeer at him, and run him out of their town. A crowd gathered and chased him. The Messenger took refuge in an orchard. Sitting in the shade of a tree, it is said that he prayed to God in the utmost contrition. "O God!" he said, "To Thee I complain of my own weakness, little resource, and lowliness before men.

O Most Merciful! Thou art the Lord of the weak, and Thou art my Lord. To whom wilt Thou confide me? To one afar who will misuse me? Or to an enemy to whom Thou hast given power over me? If Thou art not angry with me I care not. Thy favour suffices me. I take refuge in the light of Thy countenance by which the darkness is illumined, and the affairs of this world and the next are rightly ordered, lest Thy anger descend upon me or Thy wrath light upon me. It is for Thee to be satisfied until Thou art well pleased. There is no power and no might save in Thee."

It so happened that the orchard belonged to two brothers of the Makkan Quraysh, 'Utba and Shayba, who were in their garden at the time, both of whom were hostile to him and his Cause. When they saw his condition, however, they took pity on him, picked a bunch of grapes, put it in a plate and asked 'Addas, their Christian slave to take it to him. The Apostle of God thanked him and, stretching his hand to take the grapes, he said, "In the name of God," before eating. 'Addas found it unusual for an Arab, to invoke the name of God before eating, and said, "Who are you? This is not the way the people of this country act." "Where do you come from, O 'Addas?" asked the Apostle, "and what is your religion?" "I am a Christian and have come from Ninevah." replied 'Addas. Oh! From the town of the righteous Jonah son of Mattal." said the Prophet. "But how do you know about him?" asked 'Addas. The Apostle answered, "He was a Prophet, and I am a Prophet; we are brothers." 'Addas bent over and kissed his head; then He knelt and kissed his hands, and prostrating himself before him, he kissed his feet.

The two brothers were watching what was going on. One said to the other, "He's already corrupted your slave!" And when 'Addas returned to his master, he said to him, "You rascal, why did you kiss his head, hands and feet?" He told them that he was the finest man he had seen in that country; and that he knew things that only a Prophet would know. They told him, "You simpleton, don't let him beguile you into accepting his religion and giving up yours, for, by God! Your religion is better than his."

The Prophet returned to Makkah when he realized the Thaqif would not respond to God's Message. At Nakhlah, a roadside station, he rose to pray in the middle of the night. Seven men were passing by and were attracted by the words he was reciting, sat down and talked to him. When they went to their people they advised them that they had become believers. God revealed concerning them:

And when We turned aside a company of the Jinn to thee, that they might hearken to the Qur'án; and no sooner were they present at its reading than they said to each other, "Hist;" and when it was ended, they returned to their people with warnings. They said, "O our people! verily we have been listening to a Book sent down since the days of Moses, affirming the previous Scriptures; it guideth to the truth, and to the right way. O our people! Obey the Summoner of God, and believe in Him, that He may forgive your sins, and rescue you from an afflictive punishment.

Q. 46: 29-31

and again,

Say: It hath been revealed to me that a company of Jinn listened, and said, "Verily, we have heard a marvelous discourse; it guideth to the truth; wherefore we believed in it, and we will henceforth associate naught with our Lord..."

Q. 72: 1-2

THE FIRST ENCOUNTER WITH YATHRIBITES

Before re-entering the territory of Makkah, the Prophet had to seek the protection of one of the Quraysh clans, according to the custom of the time. He sought the help of a passerby who agreed to be his emissary, and who was sent to various clan chiefs to obtain their consent to protect the Apostle in Makkah so that he could convey God's Message to the people. One after the other the chiefs turned down his request. Finally, al-Mut'im, head of the clan of Nawfal[56] agreed to be his protector and sent word that he could enter the city without fear of molestation.

The last three years of the Prophet's life in Makkah, between the deaths of His uncle Abu Talib and Khadija his wife and his flight to Madinah were the most troublous years. Abu Jahl and Abu Lahab acted as watch dogs for the Quraysh, followed the Prophet's scent and countered his efforts at propagating Islám. During this period, the Messenger of God directed His attention mainly on the tribes that attended the annual fairs in Makkah, told them of his Mission, as decreed by God, recited to them parts of the Qur'án and invited them to worship the one true God, and abandon idol worship. Some responded favourably to his call, but were intimidated by the watch dogs who told them to pay no attention to such foolish and misleading innovation.

But man, however intimidating his might, can never frustrate God's Will. At the fair that year six Shaykhs, heads of the various clans of the Khazraj tribe of Yathrib met the Apostle at al-'Aqaba, listened to his discourse and a recitation of the Qur'án. Now, two factors led to their acceptance of

---

[56] He was the brother of Hashim the great grandfather of the Apostle.

Islám. Firstly, their association with the Jewish tribes that lived in Ya<u>th</u>rib. Not only had they become familiar with the Jewish Scriptures, but also whenever a dispute arose between them and the Jews, the Jews would say to them, "A Prophet will be sent soon. His day is at hand. We shall follow him and kill you by his aid as 'Ad and Iram perished." Secondly, there existed much disunity and discord among the clans of their own tribe as well as between them and the Aws, another pagan Arab tribe living in Ya<u>th</u>rib. When they heard the Apostle, therefore, they were sure that this was the Prophet the Jews had been expecting, and wished to accept him before the Jews did. They also hoped that the Prophet would bring about peace and unity within the Arab tribes and clans in Ya<u>th</u>rib.

When they returned home they invited their people to accept Islám. Soon the Apostle and Islám were familiar terms in most families in that city. They had, indeed become the talk of the town.

THE TWO PLEDGES OF AL-AQABAH

The following year, twelve Yathribites came on pilgrimage, met the Messenger of God at al-Aqaba, and swore fealty to him in accordance with the terms of the "Pledge of Women."[57] The terms were that they should associate nought with God, should not steal, nor commit adultery, refrain from killing their children, abstain from slander, and obey the Messenger in all that was right. The Apostle promised them paradise if they fulfilled their pledge, and punishment in this world, if they failed to do so, which would serve as expiation; if, however, they violated any of the terms and concealed it, then it would remain for God to decide whether to punish or to forgive on the Day of Resurrection. When the party left Makkah, the Apostle sent Mus'ab to Yathrib with instruction to read the Qur'án to them and to teach them the verities of Islám. In Yathrib, he was called "The Reader", and led the prayers since Aws and Khazraj could not bear to see a rival take the lead.

It is said that Mus'ab taught them the Friday noon congregational prayer, and taught the Faith with such fervour and vigour that Islám spread rapidly in Yathrib. It is interesting to note that when a man recognized Islám and wished to know what he was supposed to do to enter the religion, he was told to wash and purify himself and his garments, then bear witness to the truth and pray. In a very early Sura, God had revealed:

---

[57] The term implies that the intention was not the protection of the Apostle, but the practice of some of the teachings of Islám and abhorrence of pagan practices.

Thy lord — magnify Him! Thy raiment — purify it! The abomination — flee it.

Q. 74: 3-5

This is precisely what John did when he purified the Jews in the River Jordan when they confessed their sins. It is an outer and an inner purification of a person who desires to be admitted into the Faith of God.

The following year a number of the inhabitants of Yathrib went to Makkah on pilgrimage. They included both the believers in Islám and the polytheists. The believers met the Apostle in the course of the pilgrimage and agreed to meet him in the days of al-Tashriq[58] in the glen of al-Aqaba.

The Yathribite pilgrims, believers and unbelievers, slept the night together in their encampment. The believers, seventy men and two women, stole away softly when they made sure their companions were fast asleep, and went to al-Aqaba where they quietly waited for the Messenger of God. He came together with his uncle, al-'Abbas who was not a believer at the time, but who accompanied his nephew to guard him against a likely danger. Al-'Abbas spoke first warning them of the seriousness of their undertaking. "If you think that you can be faithful to what you have promised him and can protect him from his opponents, then assume the burden you have undertaken, but if you think that you will betray and abandon him after he has gone out with you, then leave him now, for he now lives in honour and safety among his people." The men said, "We have heard what you say, O al-'Abbas!" Then turning to the Apostle, they said, "You speak, O Apostle, and choose for yourself and for your Lord what you wish."

The Messenger of God recited the Qur'án and called them to God and to Islám. "I invite your allegiance." He said, "on

---

[58] The three days following the day of Sacrifice, the final rite of the pilgrim; The pilgrims should rest in Makkah these 3 days before leaving its territory.

the basis that you protect me as you would your women and children." al-Bara', the eldest and the most highly esteemed of the party took his hand and said, "By Him Who sent you with the truth we will protect you as we protect our women. We give our allegiance and we are men of war possessing arms which have been passed on from father to son." At this point, another man of the party interrupted al-Bara' and said, "O Apostle, we have ties with other men (meaning the Jews) and if we sever them perhaps when we have done that and God will have given you victory, you will return to your people and leave us?" The Apostle smiled and said, "You are of me and I am of you. I shall fight whomever you fight and make peace with whomever you make peace with." Then He asked them to elect twelve representatives from among themselves to direct their affairs. They chose nine from the tribe of Khazraj and three from Aws. Addressing the representatives, the Messenger of God said, "You are to see to your people's affairs; you are a surety for them, as the disciples were for Jesus, son of Mary, and I am for my people." They agreed to this.

Then they all approached the Apostle to clasp his hand and to swear the oath of allegiance to him. One of the Khazraj said, "O people of Khazraj, know that in swearing allegiance to this man, you are pledging yourselves to wage war against all mankind. If you think that when your wealth is exhausted by misfortune and your nobles are depleted by death you will give Him up, then stop now, for, by God, it is disgrace in this world and the next if you later abandon him; but if you think that you will remain loyal to him through adversity and misfortune, then take him, for by God it will profit you in both worlds." They all said, "We shall take him even if it brings the loss of our wealth and the killing of our nobles."

They then asked the Prophet what would be their reward if they remained faithful to him. "Paradise." he promised. They stretched their hands and swore allegiance to him. Then the

Prophet ordered them to disperse, and they returned quietly to their encampment, and later left for Madinah. By this second pledge, the Khazraj and Aws guaranteed protection to the Apostle and Islám in addition to accepting the conditions laid down in the first pledge.

THE STORY OF 'AMR'S IDOL

They returned to Madinah and openly professed Islám. In a short time, the Khazraj and Aws accepted Islám, and became known as the 'Ansar', meaning 'Helpers' as they had pledged to protect Islám. There were some old men and women, however, who found it hard to give up their pagan practices easily. 'Amr was a tribal Shaykh whose son had pledged allegiance to the Apostle in al-Aqaba, but who kept a wooden idol in his house called Manat and reverenced it. Now his son together with a few friends who had accepted Islám crept in one night, carried his idol away and threw it into a cesspit, Next day, "Amr went looking for his idol, and when he found it, he washed it, perfumed it and returned it to its place in his house. The young men, however, carried the idol away again and threw it into a cesspit, and the old Shaykh found it again, washed, cleaned and perfumed it and put it back where it belonged. This was repeated several times. Finally, 'Amr tied his sword to it, saying, "By God, I don't know who has been doing this; but if you are any good at all defend yourself with this sword."

That night when he was asleep, the men came again, untied the sword and hung a dead dog to it by a cord, took it away and cast it into a cesspit. In the morning 'Amr found the idol again with the dead dog tied to it. The people of his clan then talked with him, and he accepted Islám and became a good Muslim. He expressed his gratitude to God for opening his eyes to truth — in a few verses:

By Alláh, if you had been a god you would not have
been Tied to a dead dog in a cesspit.
Phew! that we ever treated you as a god, but now
We have found you out and left our wicked folly.
Praise be to God, Most High, the Gracious,
The Bountiful, the Provider, the Judge of all religions
Who had delivered me in time to save me
From being kept in the darkness of the grave.

FIGHTING ORDAINED: EMIGRATION TO MADINAH

When the Quraysh found out about the Apostle's compact with Khazraj and Aws, their outrage against the Apostle and the believers grew more violent. They beat the believers, most of whom were of lower classes and slaves, they dragged them by the hair when they had bushy heads, and they humiliated them by any means in their power. The believers had no choice but to bear insults and afflictions patiently, or emigrate to other lands, as the early believers had done when they went to Abyssinia, or to recant their faith.

Their stubborn rejection of God's warnings; the insolence they showed to His Messenger, accusing him of lying and imposture; their unjust and cruel treatment of the believers; their refusal to abandon their gods and believe in His unity, aroused God's wrath. He permitted warfare against injustice:

Permission is granted to those who take up arms because they have been oppressed; and verily God is well able to succour them. Those who have been driven forth from their homes wrongfully, only because they say "Our Lord is God, " ....

Q. 22: 39-40

and later:

And fight for the religion of God against those who fight against you, but transgress not (i.e. only in self defence), for God loveth not the transgressors. And kill them wherever ye find them, and turn them out of that whereof they have dispossessed you; for temptation (to idolatry) is more grievous than slaughter: yet fight not against them in the Holy Temple, until they attack you therein; but if they attack you, slay them (there). This shall be the reward of the infidels. But if they desist, God is Gracious, Merciful. Fight therefore against them, until there be no temptation (to idolatry) and the religion be God's: but if they desist, then let there be no hostility, except against the ungodly.

Q. 2: 190-193

The Messenger of God now commanded the believers to emigrate to Madinah. "The Ansar (Helpers) are your brothers in faith. They have made homes ready for you, and will receive you warmly and assist you to establish yoursleves there. God's earth is vast; one place is as good as another." Such was the Prophet's advice to the believers in Makkah. And they responded, and left individually and in groups until there remained no believer in Makkah except the Prophet, 'Alí and Abu Bakr. Several times Abu Bakr asked for permission to leave, but the Messenger of God urged him to stay, saying, "Do not do so now; perhaps God will provide a companion for you." And how Abu Bakr prayed that the Apostle would be his companion!

THE PLOT TO KILL THE MESSENGER OF GOD

The alliance of a tribe not their own, and the emigration of large numbers of the believers to Madinah alarmed the Quraysh clans. Hitherto they had been able to harass and persecute the Apostle and his followers at will, and did not feel seriously threatened by the growth of the Faith of God. Now, however, the believers were not only out of their reach, but under the protection of the tribes of Khazraj and Aws. They were, moreover, to inhabit an important station on the Makkah-Syria trade route and could easily pose a major threat to their vital commercial interests. They feared the consequence of the events that were developing. They were also certain that the Prophet would soon join his followers in Madinah.

The chiefs of the various Quraysh clans gathered in the House of Assembly, where important decisions were usually taken, to deliberate on the proper course of action to take next to uproot what they considered to be a life-threatening cancer. Several suggestions were put forth. One suggested to lock up the Apostle, keep him in fetters until death would overtake him, as it happened to Zuhayr and other poets before him; another advised his expulsion and banishment.

An old Shaykh from Najd who had joined them at the Assembly counselled them against such imprudent measures. Finally, Abu Jahl came up with an idea that found general approval. A strong, well-born young man from each clan would be armed with a sharp sword. They would collectively attack the Apostle at night when He was asleep in his bed and kill him. The Banu Hashim, who had vowed to protect the Apostle, could not wage war against all the other clans. The best they could do under the circumstances would be to demand blood money which could easily be paid. Having agreed on this plan, they dispersed.

But God had a different plan for His Messenger. He now permitted him to emigrate to Madinah. Accounts that have come down to us regarding his flight generally agree on the main events and places, but are slightly different in details. We know that he asked 'Alí his son-in-law to stay behind to settle his accounts and return to their proper owners all that they had entrusted to him for safe-keeping for his honesty, his integrity and his unblemished character had rendered him trustee of many Makkans. We also know that Abu Bakr was his companion on the journey, together with 'Amir, a Muslim and a freedman of Abu Bakr, who served them, as well as a hired guide who was a polytheist. We know that they spent three days and three nights in a cave called <u>Th</u>awr, just south of Makkah, that 'Abdullah, Abu Bakr's son, brought them news — daily of what was happening in Makkah and that Abu Bakr's daugther Asma' brought them their travelling provisions upon leaving the cave. We also know that they were guided on a route along the Red Sea shore northwards to Madinah and that they reached Quba', a district in the south of that city at noon on an intensely hot Monday, September 24, A.D. 622, and that they were welcomed by a large number of the Muhajirin and the Ansar (The Emigrants and the Helpers).

To return now to the plot to kill the Messenger of God, the young members of the clans went one night to the Prophet's house, but found 'Alí occupying the bed. They asked him the whereabouts of the Apostle and when he professed ignorance, beat him up and left him. 'Alí stayed in Makkah three more days, returned all the deposits and joined the Apostle of God in Madinah and lodged with him.

Concerning the plots of Quray<u>sh</u>, God revealed:

Or they say: he is a poet, one for whom we may await some adverse turn of fortune. Say, await! Verily I am with you among those who await.

Q. 52: 30-31

And when the unbelievers plotted against thee, that they might either detain thee, or put thee to death, or expel thee: they plot, and God plots; and God is the best of plotters.

Q. 8: 30

SOME EVENTS OF THE FIRST YEAR IN MADINAH

For thirteen years, since he was dignified by God to be His Messenger, Muhammad endured the persecution and humiliation inflicted upon him and his followers by the Makkans with the utmost patience and resignation, and swerved not, in the least, from the course commanded by God. When Abu Jahl threatened to set his foot on his neck if he saw him in the act of prostration, God revealed:

> ... Obey him not; but adore God; and draw nigh (unto Him).
>
> Q. 96: 19

And on other occasions, He sent down these verses:

> Verily, We have sent down unto thee the Qur'án, a Revelation; Wherefore patiently await the judgment of thy Lord, and obey not any wicked or unbeliever among them.
>
> Q. 76: 23-24

> Say: Verily I fear, if I should rebel against my Lord, the punishment of the great day ...
>
> Q. 6: 15

These and many similar admonitions of his Lord, Muhammad adhered to meticulously no matter how his enemies ridiculed and scoffed at him causing him pain and suffering.

But now, amidst the believers — both the Emigrants and the Madinites — he felt safe and secure, and could pursue God's will in establishing a well-ordered Muslim community and in unifying the feuding tribes in the recognition of one

God and in the obedience to His laws and ordinances. This was, by no means, an easy task. At the time Muhammad entered Madinah, several clans and sub-clans of the two main tribes, the Khazraj and the Aws lived in that city. The Khazraj was by far wealthier and more important than the Aws. Both had been weakened through petty rivalries. With the exception of a few such clans of the Aws tribe who remained heathen, all had accepted Islám. The Makkan Muslims had emigrated to the city, and had to be lodged and fed until they could find employment. This was a severe burden on the 'Helpers' who had to support them from their meagre resources. Three Jewish tribes, the Banu Qaynuqa', the Banu al-Nadir, and the Banu Qurayza also resided in their settlements in the city, the former did not own agricultural land, but were mostly goldsmiths, the latter two owned date palm orchards.

The first task of Muhammad was to draw up a document, later called the Constitution of Madinah, a sort of agreement that delineated the reciprocal obligations of these various entities. It is a lengthy document, the main features of which are: (1) God is one and Muhammad is His Apostle; (2) Muslims of Quraysh and Yathrib and those who follow them and labour with them are one community (Umma) to the exclusion of all men; (3) regulations governing forays and campaigns against God's enemies, such as obligation to make collective peace, avenging the blood of one another shed in the way of God, fair and equitable conditions for all, etc. etc.; (4) the illegality of helping and sheltering evil-doers[59]; (5) the obligation to refer all differences and disputes to God and to the Apostle; (6) Yathrib was declared a sanctuary for all the contracting parties who were henceforth bound to help one another against attacks; (7) loyalty was stressed and

---

[59] The Arabic word used is Muhdith, which could apply to adultery and ritual impurity.

treachery severely condemned; (8) the Jews were given the same protection they had enjoyed before, their rights guaranteed, but were expected to show loyalty and to pay dues along with the believers as long as hostilities lasted. These were some of the provisions of the Covenant. Certain sentences were repeated and are quoted here owing to their importance: "Loyalty is a protection against treachery;" "God accepts what is nearest to piety and goodness in this document," "God approves of this document. This deed will not protect the unjust and the sinner;" and "If any dispute or controversy likely to cause trouble should arise it must be referred to God and to Muhammad the Apostle of God." For the next ten years until his death, the Prophet was the legislator, the judge, the arbiter, the statesman, the commander in chief, the leader, but, above all God's spokesman and representative on earth and all these offices and functions he performed strictly under His direction and command. When the Apostle of God entered Yathrib, naturally each of the clans wished that he would settle in its quarters. Some have reported that the Prophet let loose the reins of the camel he was riding to signify that he would abide by God's will. The camel went along and stopped briefly in turn at the quarters of several of the clans each of whom invited the Prophet and begged him to stay with them. But the Prophet said, "Let her go her way." Finally the camel came to the home of Banu Malik b. al-Najjar and stopped in an open space used for drying dates and knelt there. But the Prophet did not dismount. The camel rose, went a short distance and returned to where it had knelt before and knelt there again putting its chest upon the ground, a sign of fatigue. The Messenger of God alighted, enquired about the open space and was told that it belonged to two orphans, Sahl and Suhayl. He agreed to pay them its price and ordered a mosque to be built there together with houses for himself. And until these were completed, he stayed with a believer. The Muslims, particularly the Emigrants, undertook the task.

The Apostle joined them frequently to encourage them to work harder. As soon as the mosque was ready the Friday noon congregational prayer was observed, and the Prophet delivered sermons, praising and glorifying God, imploring His aid, calling upon the believers to love God with all their hearts and love one another in the spirit of God, admonishing them to worship God and associate naught with Him, to fear Him as He ought to be feared, to beware breaking His covenant as this would arouse His wrath and to act loyally towards God and shun hypocracy. He also told them that on the day they find themselves in the presence of their Lord only kindly speech and good deeds will be rewarded.

To fortify the bond of fellowship between the Emigrants and the Helpers, the Prophet asked each to adopt a brother for the sake of God. He himself raised 'Alí's hand and declared him a brother. Abu Bakr, 'Umar, Hamza and others adopted brothers from among the 'Helpers'. Islám was now firmly established in Madinah.[60]

It was necessary to devise means for summoning the believers to the mosque for the observance of prayers at appointed times. The Jews were called to their synagogues by the use of a trumpet. The Prophet preferred a clapper for the purpose. One of the believers then had a dream which he recounted to the Apostle, saying: "A phantom visited me in the night. There passed by me a man wearing two green garments carrying a clapper in his hand, and I asked him to sell it to me. When he asked me what I wanted it for I told him that it was to summon people to prayer, whereupon he offered to show me a better way: it was to say thrice Alláh-u-Akbar, I bear witness that there is no God but Alláh; I bear witness that Muhammad is the Apostle of God. Come to

---

[60] The original name of the city, Yathrib, was changed to Madinah, abbreviated from 'Madinat, un, Nabi' meaning the city of the Prophet.

[61] The Arabic word 'Falah' means salvation, prosperity.

prayer. Come to Prayer. Come to divine service[61]. Come to divine service. Alláh-u-Akbar, Alláh-u-Akbar. There is no God but Alláh.' "

The Apostle considered this a true vision and Bilal, who had a powerful, penetrating voice, was ordered to cry the words from the highest roof top in Madinah and summon the believers to prayer. Bilal was thus honoured to be the first Muezzin in Islám, and that same formula has been used to this day by all the Sunni and Shi'ah Muezzins throughout the world, calling the believers from the top of minarets.[62] With the introduction of loudspeakers the voice now reverberates over a much wider area in towns and cities where Muslims live.

Seven or eight months after his arrival at Madinah, the Messenger of God consummated his marriage to 'A'isha. They had been betrothed in Makkah two years earlier, when she was seven years old, and after the death of Khadija his first wife. When he came to Madinah, he had only one wife, Sauda, a widow who had a son named 'Abdu'l-Rahman, and who had emigrated to Abyssinia with her husband Sakran. 'A'isha was Muhammad's third wife. All his marriages after Khadija had been contracted for reasons of compassion and protection as well as to cement relationships with close friends or to establish union with tribes.

Minor forays took place in the first year of the Prophet's stay in Madinah. These were led by Hamzih, 'Ubaydah, and Sa'd with small contingents to intercept the caravans of Quraysh. No fighting took place and no booty was taken. The Messenger of God, also let three expeditions personally. The first known as the Expedition on Buwat was intended to

---

[62] The Shi'ah call to prayer has additions: after 'Muhammad is the Apostle of God,' comes 'I bear witness that 'Alí is the friend of Alláh,; after the 2nd cry 'Come to divine service,' is chanted twice 'Come to the best work'.

be a raid on the Quraysh, but He returned to Madinah without any encounter with them. The second resulted in signing a treaty of friendship with the Banu Mudlit and their confederates Banu Damrah. The third was punitive in nature against Kurz who had raided and gone away with the pasturing camels of Madinah, but Kurz eluded him and escaped.

THE JEWS RECOGNIZE THE PROPHET: FEW ACCEPT HIM

'Abdullah b. Salam was a learned rabbi who recognized the Apostle as soon as he heard of him. His name, the time of his appearance and the description of his words and deeds all corresponded with the prophecies of the Scriptures. But he did not share his feelings with anyone until the Apostle came to Madinah. He was tending to his palm trees one day when he heard that Muhammad was in Quba'. "Alláh-u-Akbar," he cried from the top of the palm tree. His aunt, who was squatting below, said, "Good gracious! If you had heard that Moses had returned you could not have made more fuss!" "Indeed, Aunt," he said, "He is the brother of Moses and follows his religion and has come with the same Mission." "Is He really the prophet that we are expecting to come at this very time?" she asked. "Assuredly He is," he answered. He came down the palm tree, went to the Apostle and became a Muslim. He then returned home and ordered his family to accept Islám, too.

He kept his faith secret from the Jews, and told the Apostle that if he revealed the matter to them they would bring accusations against him. "Call the Jews," he asked the Apostle, "and find out my status among them while I hide in a room in your house." The Prophet invited the leaders of the Jews and asked them about 'Abdullah's standing among them. "He is our chief, and the son of our chief, our rabbi, and our learned man," they all declared. 'Abdullah then emerged from his hiding place and said, "Fear God, O Jews, and accept what He has sent you. For by God, you know that He is the Apostle of God. You will find him described in the Torah and even named. I testify that he is the Apostle of God; I believe in him, hold him to be true, and acknowledge him." They accused him of lying, called down curses upon him and left. He then proclaimed his faith publicly; his family and his aunt K̲h̲alidah followed suit.

Mukhayriq was another learned rabbi who was attracted to God and His Messenger. He was a wealthy man. The Battle of Uhud, in the third year of the Hijrah, fell on the sabbath. Mukhayriq urged the Jews to help Muhammad, as bound by their contract, but they refused on the plea that it was the sabbath of the Lord. "Accursed be your sabbath!" He cried, and followed the Prophet to the battlefield. He told his people: "If I am killed my property is to go to Muhammad to be spent as God directs him." He was killed in the battle. The Apostle distributed his property to the needy in Madinah, and, as some have reported, he used to say, "Mukhayriq is the best of the Jews."

And from Safiya, a Jewess comes this story: "I was the favourite child of my father and my uncle Abu Yasir. When I was present they took no notice of their other children. When Muhammad was staying in Quba', the two went to see him at dawn and did not return until after night-fall, weary, worn out, drooping and feeble. I went up to them in childish pleasure as I always did, and they were so sunk in gloom that they took no notice of me. I heard my uncle say to my father, 'Is he he? Do you recognize him, and can you be sure?' 'Yes! And what do you feel about him?' 'By God I shall be his enemy as long as I live!' "[63]

---

[63] Then shall two be in the field; the one shall be taken, and the other left. Matt. 24: 40; Luke 17:34.

THE JEWS AND THE HYPOCRITES

Although the Messenger of God enjoyed considerably more freedom of action among the 'Emigrants' and the 'Helpers' in Madinah and felt better protected and secure from the venomous tongues of the Makkan Quraysh, yet he had to contend firstly with the hostility of the Jewish rabbis who were jealous and filled with malice because God had chosen His Messenger from among the pagan Arabs, and secondly with the duplicity and the machinations of the hypocrites (Munafiqin) who pretended to be Muslims because their people had accepted Islám but in truth clung to their heathenistic beliefs and despised the Apostle and his new ways and teachings. And when these two joined hands they posed a formidable adversary to the Apostle and an obstacle to his reforms and his efforts to create unity among the tribes. They tried by every means to seduce the believers from obeying the Apostle, dissuaded them from taking an active role in fighting in defence of the community, and, in violation of the terms of the constitution of Madinah, betrayed the Muslim community by acting as spies for the Makkan Quraysh, promising them their support in case they attacked the Muslims. There were instances, though rare, of the Hypocrites participating in the battles on the side of the Apostle, then turning against the Muslims by going over to the Quraysh. Such a treacherous behaviour could not be tolerated by a community which was weaker than its adversary in numbers, equipment and material resources.

The Qur'án is replete with admonitions and exhortations to the Jews and the Hypocrites. A few will be quoted below to give the reader a clearer insight into the matter:

When God entered into covenant with the prophets, He said, "This is the Book and the Wisdom which I give you. Hereafter shall a prophet come unto you to confirm the Scriptures already with you. Ye shall surely believe on him, and ye shall surely aid him. Are you resolved?" They said, "We are resolved;" "Be ye then the witnesses," said He, "and I will be a witness as well as you. And whoever turneth back after this, these are surely the perverse. Do they desire any other religion but God's? ...

> Q.3: 81-83

It is generally admitted that the first hundred verses in the second Sura of the Qur'án, 'The Cow,' were revealed in reference to the Jewish Rabbis and the hypocrites:

And some there are who say, "We believe in God, and in the Last Day;" Yet they are not believers! Fain would they deceive God and the believers; and only themselves they deceive, and they are not aware. In their hearts is a disease, and God has increased that disease. Their's a sore chastisement for that they lie. And when it is said unto them, "Cause not mischief in the land." they say, "We are the peacemakers: Truly, they are the mischief-makers. But they perceive it not! And when it is said to them, "Believe as the people believe," they say, "Shall we believe as the fools believe?" Truly, they are the fools, but they do not know. And when they meet those who believe, they say, "We believe;" and when they meet privately with their Satans, they say, "We are with you; we were only mocking: God shall mock them and keep them long in their rebellion, wandering blindly in their errors. These are they who have purchased error at the price of guidance; but their traffic has not been gainful, nor are they guided. They are like one who kindleth a fire, and when it has thrown its light all about him... God taketh away their light and leaveth them in darkness — they cannot see! Deaf, dumb, blind — so they shall not return. Or like a storm-cloud out of the Heaven, big with darkness, thunder and lightning; they thrust their fingers into their ears because of the thunder-clap, for fear of death! And God encompasses the unbelievers; The lightning almost snatches away their sight; so oft as it gleameth on them, they walk in it, but when darkness is over them, they halt; had God willed, He would have taken away their hearing and their sight. Truly, God is powerful over everything.

Q. 2: 8-20

When the hypocrites come to thee, they say, "We bear witness that thou art the Messenger of God." God knoweth that thou art His Messenger, and God testifieth that the hypocrites are certainly liars. Under the shelter of their faith, they turn aside others from the way of God! It is surely evil what they do. This because they believed, then disbelieved. Therefore their hearts are sealed and they understand not. When thou seest them, their persons please thee; and when they speak, thou listeneth to their discourse (with delight). Like timbers are they serving as a prop,[64] they imagine every cry to be against them; they are enemies — beware of them then. May God destroy them! How false are they! And when it is said to them, "Come, the Messenger of God will ask pardon for you." they turn their heads aside, and thou seest them bloated with pride. Alike shall it be to them whether thou ask forgiveness for them, or ask it not. By no means will God forgive them; Verily, God will not guide unrighteous people. These are they who say (to the Ansar, the Helpers), "Spend not on those who are with the Apostle of God (meaning the Emigrants, the Muhajirin) so that they may leave him." Yet the treasures of the heavens and of the earth are God's! But he hypocrites do not understand! They say,

---

[64] 'Khushub-un Musannadatun' has been translated by the Guardian in the Iqán 'Pompous and hypocritical' p. 164.

"If we return to Madinah, the mightier will surely drive out the weaker therefrom." But might belongs to God and to His Messenger, and to the believers. Yet the hypocrites know it not.

Q. 63: 1-8

and yet again:

There are some men who say, "We believe in God," but when afflicted for God's sake, he esteemeth the persecution of men as the punishment of God. Yet if success cometh from thy Lord, they say, "Verily we are with you: Doth not God well know that which is in the breasts of (His) creatures? Verily God well knoweth the true believers, and He well knoweth the hypocrites. The unbelievers say unto those who believe. "Follow our way, and we will bear your sins." Howbeit they shall not bear any part of their sins: for they are liars.

Q. 29: 10-12

A DEPUTATION FROM THE CHRISTIANS OF NAJRAN

Sixty riders including fourteen chiefs, led by 'Aqib, their temporal leader, and Abu Haritha, their Bishop and spiritual leader, came to the Messenger of God. While on their way to Madinah, the mule upon which the Bishop was riding stumbled. His brother Kuz said, "Cursed be so and so!" meaning the Prophet. "Don't say that; by God, He is the Prophet we have been waiting for," said the Bishop. Kuz said, "If you know that, brother, what stops you from accepting him?" The Bishop replied, "The way people treat us makes it impossible for me to accept him. You see they give us titles, gifts and contribution, and hold us in high esteem. They oppose Muhammad If I accept him, I shall lose all these favours." Kuz was saddened by his brother's attitude and pondered much about man's heedlessness, until he became a Muslim and told this story.

The people sat with the Prophet and asserted that God could not be one since, they argued, if He were one He would not say, "We have created and We have decreed." He would rather have said, "I have created, I have decreed." The Messenger of God invited them to submit. They declared that they had already submitted. The Apostle told them, "Not so. You say that God has a son, you worship the cross and you eat pork; therefore you have not submitted to the one true God." They said, "But tell us, Muhammad, who was the father of Jesus?" The first sixty-four verses of the third Sura, 'The Family of 'Imrán were revealed then in reply to their question; A few I shall quote below. The rest I shall recommend to the reader to study:

V. 2   There is no God but God, the Living, the Self-Subsisting!

V. 3   He hath sent down unto thee the Book with trust, confirming that which was (revealed) before it;

V. 4   For He had formerly sent down the Torah and the Gospel, a guidance unto men; and He also sent down the Furqan. [65]

V. 65   Verily those who believe not the signs of God, shall suffer a grievous punishment.

V. 42   And when the angels said. O Mary, verily God hath chosen thee, and hath purified thee above the women of the world.

V. 43   O Mary, be obedient to thy Lord, and prostrate thyself and bow down with those who bow.

V. 45   When the angel said, O Mary! Verily God sendeth thee good tidings, the Word from Himself; his name shall be Messiah Jesus the son of Mary, illustrious of this world and in the next, and one of those who have near access to God.

V. 59   Verily, Jesus is as Adam in the sight of God. He created him of dust; He then said to him, Be, and he was.

V. 61   To those who dispute with thee about this matter after the knowledge that has come to thee, say: Come, let us summon our sons and your sons, our wives and your wives, and ourselves and yourselves. Then will we invoke and lay the malison of God on those that lie.

V. 64   Say: O people of the Book! Come ye to a just judgment between us and you—That we worship not aught but God, and that we join no other god

---

[65] This word has been translated 'discrimination,' 'distinction', illumination' by various translators. It implies guidance which make one distinguish between right and wrong. It is the title of the 25th Surah of the Qur'án.

with Him, and that the one of us take not the other for lords[66], beside God. Then if they turn their backs, Say: Bear ye witness that we are Muslims[67].

Thus God invited them to fairness and justice and counselled them against endless and futile argumentation, and suggested a decisive way to settle the matter between them by invoking the judgment of God and His curse on those that lie. They consulted their chief leader 'Aqib. He told them: "O Christians, you know well that Muhammad is God's Messenger and has pronounced His declaration concerning the nature of our Lord Jesus Christ. Such invocation to God would be in his favour and our destruction. If you are determined to cling to your religion and to retain your belief in the doctrine of the Sonship of your Lord, take leave of Muhammad and go home." So they came to the Apostle, told him of their decision not to abandon their religion and not to resort to invoking God's malison. They asked him, however, to send a trusted man to settle some financial matters in dispute among them. The Apostle chose Abu 'Ubayda b. al-Jarrah and ordered him to go with them and judge between them faithfully in all matters in dispute among them.

---

[66] As the Christians treat their bishops and priets. See St. John 5: 43-44

[67] i.e. resigned to the Will of God.

THE SURA AL-BAQARAH—THE COW

During the second year of the Apostle's stay in Madinah, momentous events took place. The main portion of the Sura, entitled "The Cow", the longest and the most important Chapter of the Qur'án was revealed at this time. Owing to the significance of this Sura which, indeed, represents the essence of Islám and its teachings and ordinances, it is analyzed here in greater detail.

1. Verses 2-5, 177[68], 186, 195, 215, 219, Articles of Faith: No doubt is there about this Book (the Qur'án): It is a guidance unto the God-Fearing, who believe in the Unseen, observe prayer, give out in charity, believe in the Revelations sent to the Apostle of God, and to the Ones before him, and have firm assurance in the life to come.

2. Verses 6-30 reveal the status of the unbeliever and the hypocrites.

3. Verses 21-29, 163-167: The unity of God, the Creator, the Knower. The physical elements in nature — earth, heaven, rain and fruit for sustenance — can also symbolically reflect man's heart and mind, religion, the Word of God which produces moral values for the spiritual growth of man. Verse 23 challenges the doubters to produce a Sura like it[69]. Verse 29, might also refer to the creation of the physical world, and the

---

[68] See the Iqán, pp. 92-93 for the explanation of the 'Last Day' mentioned in this verse "... but he is pious who believeth in God and the Last Day..." The promise of the 'Last Day' has been mentioned in the Qur'án in 28 verses.

[69] See Iqán p. 204-205.

seven heavens (religions in the Adamic Cycle—
Adam — Noah — Abraham — Moses — Jesus —
Muhammad, and the Báb).

4. Man's need for guidance: appointment of Messengers:
    Verses 30-39 Adam is commissioned to be God's
    Messenger. Angels are the believers who obey him;
    Satan (Iblis) represents those who oppose him. The
    Garden represents the Faith, the Religion, the
    Revelation, sent down by God. Whoever believes and
    obeys is the dweller of the Garden. The unbeliever is
    in the Fire, a condition, a mess he has created for
    himself. Verse 38 is God's covenant with man, a
    promise not to leave him to his own devices, but
    to send him guidance and declares that whoever
    follows His guidance will not come to grief, but
    the unbelievers will be the companions of the Fire.

5. Verses 40-141[70], 211. The Jews are mainly
    addressed, though some verses relate to the
    Christians. They are called the People of the Book
    because they had received Scriptures before.
    Verses 114, 115, 118, 119 are addressed to the
    Quraysh.

---

[70] a. concerning explanation of vs. 2:46 and 2:249 To wit: They who bear
in mind that they shall attain unto the presence of their Lord, and that
unto Him shall they retrun.

They who held it as certain that they must meet God, said, 'How oft,
by God's will, hath a small host vanquished a numerous host.' see
Iqán pp. 138, 139, and 169, 170.

b. concerning "Perversion of the Text" verses 75, and 79, see the Iqán,
pp. 86-88.

c. concerning clinging to verses that support one's argument and
rejecting the part contrary to one's desire as stated in v. 85, see the
Iqán p. 169.

d. concerning verse 87, see Iqán pp. 13 and 71.

e. concerning verse 89, see Iqán p. 150.

f. concerning verse 94, see Iqán p. 227.

g. concerning verse 115, see Iqán p. 52.

Verses 142-152. Change of the Qiblah (Point of Adoration) from Jerusalem to the Ka'bah (Sacred Mosque in Makkah).[71]

Verses 153-167, 174-176. Miscellaneous injunctions: Patience in tests and trials; Martyrdom in the path of God is a renewal of life; circumambulation of Safa and Marwah is a rite of pilgrimage; cursed be he who conceals Revelations or fails to present them in their prisitine purity, but if such a person repents, amends and reveals what he has concealed, God will forgive him; the curse of God, His angels and all men will be on one who dies an unbeliever.

Verses 168, 172, 173. Clean and forbidden food.

Verses 178-179-194. Laws concerning retaliation.

Verses 180-182. Laws concerning the writing of a Will.

Verses 183-187. The ordinance of Fasting.

Verses 188. Illegal acquisition of another's wealth and recourse to judges to justify such acquisition to ease one's conscience.

Verses 189. New moon indicates times and the month of pilgrimage[72]. Enter houses from the front door not from the back window.

Verses 190-193, 196, 216-217, 243-252. Fighting.

Verses 197-203. Ordinances concerning Pilgrimage.

Verses 204-209. Mischief-makers and peace-makers.

Verse 210. The promise of the Day of Resurrection

---

[71] Refer to the Iqán, pp. 49-52.

[72] See Iqán p. 182.

when God shall come down in the shadow of the clouds with angles[73].

Verse 212. Love of the world (materialism) cause of disbelief in God. The God-fearing shall be superior to the worldly-minded on the Day of Resurrection,

Verse 213. Mankind was of one Faith; Apostles brought God's message of guidance; those to whom clear evidence was given disputed with each other out of mutual envy: God directs believers to the right way.

Verses 214, 218. Only the long-suffering enter the Garden (God's religion).

Verse 219. Prohibition of intoxicants and games of chance.

Verse 220. Righteous dealing with orphans.

Verse 221. Marriage with idolatresses and idolaters forbidden unless they become Muslims.

Verse 222. Sexual intercourse while a woman is in her course is forbidden until she is cleansed.

Verse 223. Conjugal relations is for procreation, should be preceded by acts elevating the soul and the recognition that one will meet his Lord.

Verses 224-226. Make not God the object of your oaths that ye will deal justly, and be devout, and make peace among men.[74]

---

[73] See the Iqán pp. 75 and 144.

[74] According to pre-Islámic custom, men could swear by God to separate themselves from their wives, freeing themselves from marital obligations. Islám forbids this.

Verses 227-231. Ordinances concerning Divorce.[75]

Verse 233. Suckling of Babies; parent's rights and duties in this respect.

Verses 234-235. Right of widows to remarry, and to a year's residence and maintenance if they remain unmarried.

Verses 236-237. Provision for divorced women when marriage has not been consummated.

Verses 238-239. Ordinances concerning observance of prayer.

Verses 241-242. Provision to be made for divorced women.

Verse 253. Station of the Messenger of God; preference of some before others; Jesus was strengthened with the Holy Spirit. If God had pleased, their followers would not have contended among themselves.

Verses 254, 261-274. Material sacrifice in the path of God, and the qualities of charity and giving.

Verse 255. Attributes of the Almighty.

Verses 256, 257. No complusion in religion; God has made clear right and wrong, individual choice, reward and punishment.

Verses 258-260. Similies to show the meaning of the raising of the dead.

Verses 275-282. Prohibition of usury.

---

[75] It was customary for a man's relatives to live with him. The phrase, "without turning them out," means that the relatives could not send the widow out of the residence immediately after the death of her husband.

Verses 282, 283. Obligation to write contracts in monetary and business transactions; fear ye God; God will teach you.[76]

Verse 284. God is the possessor of the Heavens and the Earth; He doeth what He pleaseth; He knoweth what man reveals and what he conceals; He is the All-Powerful.

Verse 285. The Apostle believes in the Revelations sent down to him from his Lord, as do the faithful who believe in God, His Angels, His Books, and His Apostles: We make no distinction between any of His Apostles[77]. Test of faith is: "We have heard, and we obey[78]. God's mercy is sought since all return to Him."

Verse 286. God lays not a burden on any soul beyond his strength; every soul reaps the product of his labour; a prayer and supplication to God.

---

[76] See the Iqán, p. 69.

[77] For the apparent discrepancy between this statement and that in verse 253, see the Iqán pp. 104, 152, 176, 177. Read also verse 136 in this Surah.

[78] See the Iqán, p. 111.

THE BATTLE AT BADR

The encounter which took place at Badr, a valley eighty-five miles South West of Madinah, between the Apostle who led 310 believers of both the 'Emigrants' and the 'Helpers', and the Quraysh who rallied a thousand strong to protect their endangered caravan, returning from Syria laden with merchandise and other valuables, was another very important event of the second year of the Prophet's stay in Madinah.

It must be remembered that the Madinans had to support, with their meagre resources, a considerable number of families who had emigrated from Makkah. The emigrants had been forced to leave their homes because of the harsh and cruel treatment of the Quraysh. Conditions in Madinah were indeed extremely hard. Men, women and children were living on subsistence ration of dates. They were forced to go out foraging. Any booty would be welcome. It is said that when the Apostle was informed that the Caravan was returning to Makkah, led by Abu-Sufyan and guarded by thirty to forty men, he gave permission to whoever desired to raid the caravan. "Perhaps God will give it as a prey, "he told them. Some were eager to do that, some hesitated, not certain of the Prophet's intention to go to war. Abu-Sufyan got wind of this and, alarmed and worried, dispatched a hired messenger to Makkah to warn to Quraysh of the danger to their wealth and property. And when he reached the vicinity of Badr, his inquiries indicated the nearness of the enemy and he re-routed the caravan to the sea-shore track southward to Makkah, avoiding a skirmish.

The Prophet set out in the month of Ramadan. The party had seventy camels which they shared in turn; They had no cavalry and had poor equipment. He took the road to Makkah, but turned westward, leaving the road to his left, and proceeded towards Badr. He was not sure of ; the support he would get from the bulk of his companions who were of the Supporters, the Madinans. Their pledge at al-'Aqaba was to protect him as they would their wives and children in their own city of Madinah. But now they were out of their territory. He stopped at a station on the way to Badr and sought their advice. His mind was put to rest when Sa'd b. Mu'adh, a spokesman of the Ansar (the supporters) got up and said, 'We believe in you, we declare your truth and we witness that what you have brought is the truth, and we have given you our word and agreement to hear and obey; so go where you wish, we are with you; and by God, if you were to ask us to cross this sea and you plunged into it, we would plunge into it with you; not a man would stay behind. We do not dislike the idea of meeting your enemy tomorrow. We are experienced in war, trustworthy in combat. It may well be that God will let us show you something which will bring you joy, so take us along with God's blessing. Heartened by Sa'd's words, He said, 'Forward in good heart, for God has promised me one of the two parties[79], and by God, it is as though I have already seen the enemy lying prostrate.'

When they reached Badr, the Prophet stopped at the well nearest Madinah. Al-Hubab approached him and said, 'Is this a place which God has ordered you to occupy, so that we can neither advance nor withdraw from it, or is it a matter of opinion and military tactics?' When he learned that no divine Revelation had descended in that respect, he pointed out that it was an unsuitable location, and suggested that they occupy the farthest well, build a cistern near it, fill it with water and cap all the wells in their rear so that the enemy may have no access to water. The Apostle agreed and action was taken accordingly.

---

[79] By the two parties is meant the Caravan or the Quraysh army. Reflection on the Revelation (8: 7, 8) shows clearly that God's purpose was not a raid on the Caravan for material gains, but a victory for Islám and the establishment of the truth of the Cause of God.

Meanwhile the Quraysh had mustered a force of about a thousand men and hurried towards Madinah to protect the on-coming Caravan. They encamped south of the hill 'Aqanqal. A messenger arrived from Abu-Sufyan, the leader of the Caravan, informing them that the Caravan had by-passed Muhammad's men and was safe. He advised them to return to Makkah as their object had been achieved. At that time contention arose in the Quraysh camp. Some leaders thought nothing would be gained by fighting as most of the Emigrants were close relatives of the Makkan Quraysh, and they would always be remembered as killing their own kith and kin. 'Utba was a leader of the Quraysh who was averse to fighting. One of his own sons was a Muslim and one in the Muslim camp. He stood up and said, 'O people of Quraysh! By God, you will gain naught by giving battle to Muhammad and his companions. If you fall upon him, each one of you will always be looking with loathing on the face of another who has slain the son of his paternal or maternal uncle or some man of his kin...'

But they could not prevail on Abu Jahl. When he heard 'Utba, he cried with anger, "No, by God, we will not turn back until God decides between us and Muhammad." He accused 'Utba of cowardice and added, "His son is among them, so he is afraid lest you slay him." He incited 'Amir b. al-Hadrami, whose brother had been killed by the Muslims in a previous expedition at Nakhla, to seek blood revenge, although 'Utba, his ally and protector agreed to pay blood-money if they returned without fighting. Even Addas urged his masters, 'Utba and Shayba, not to engage in battle against Muhammad[80]. But in the end the party of Abu Jahl prevailed.

Rain poured down that night, less in the valley where the Apostle and his companions had encamped, hardening the soft sand under their feet to ease their movement, far more

---

[80] Do you remember Addas in the story, 'The Apostle Goes to al-Ta'if to convey God's message to the Thaqif'? If you don't, read it again.

intensely on the Quraysh side, rendering their movement over the sand-hill 'Aqanqal arduous and fatiguing. The Apostle kept his ranks close and forbade them to advance until he would give the orders. And when he saw the enemy descending from the hill, he cried, 'O God, here come the Quraysh in their vanity and pride, contending with Thee and calling Thy Apostle a liar. O God! grant the help which Thou didst promise me. Destroy them this morning!'

A few men of the Quraysh approached the cistern to drink water. All were killed. One who had sworn to drink crawled towards the cistern and drank of the water, but was struck by Hamzih's sword and was killed in the cistern. The two brothers 'Utba and Shayba and Walid, 'Utba's son, wounded by Abu Jahl's imputation of cowardice, advanced and challenged three of Muhammad's companions to single combat. Three responded, but were arrogantly rejected as they were not considered their equal in rank and birth. Muhammad said, "Ye sons of Hashim! Arise and fight according to your right." Hamzih, 'Alí and 'Ubayda, uncle and cousins of the Apostle went forth. Walid and 'Alí, the youngest of the six were the first to engage in battle. The encounter was swift. Walid was mortally wounded by 'Alí's sword. Shayba then engaged Hamzih, and was soon slain by the latter's sword. 'Utba and 'Ubayda then entered the field. They were the oldest of the six. Swords clashed and gleamed. At last a blow from 'Utba's sword cut 'Ubayda's leg and he fell to the ground. 'Alí and Hamzih rushed on 'Utba and killed him. 'Ubayda died, a martyr three days later. This early and swift defeat of their heroes dampened the spirit of the Quraysh, but lifted the courage of their adversaries. The battle-cry was raised. It is said that the Apostle took a handful of pebbles and, turning towards the Quraysh, said, 'Foul be those faces!' Then he cast the pebbles at them and ordered his companions to charge. The ranks closed and the fighting became general. The Prophet asked the Muslims to spare his uncle al-'Abbas and Abu'l-Bakhtari. The former had been forced to fight against his will; the latter had never insulted the Prophet and his companions, had shown kindness to him in Makkah, and had been among those who repealed the boycott there.

The Quraysh were routed. Many of their chiefs were slain, and their nobles became captives. Accounts of the number of the Quraysh slain and the captives are varied, from 49 killed and 49 taken prisoners to 70 killed and 70 taken captives. The Muslims lost 14 'Emigrants' and 8 'Helpers' (Ansar). In their hasty retreat, the Quraysh abandoned their armour, beasts of burden, camp and equipage. The dead of the Quraysh were thrown into a pit and covered with stones and gravel. Standing by the pit, the Messenger of God called the names of the buried one by one and said "O people of the pit! You were an evil kinsfolk to your Prophet. You called me a liar when others believed me; you cast me out when others took me in; you fought against me when others fought on my side," then He added, "Have you found what your Lord promised you to be true? For I have found what my Lord promised me to be true." Some of the companions standing nearby wondered why the Apostle was talking to dead people. He said, "They know that what I promised them is the truth, but they cannot answer me."

When 'Utba's corpse was being dragged into the pit, the Apostle, turning to his son, Abu Hudhayfah, said a few words of sympathy. He replied that his sorrow was due to the fact that he always considered his father to be a wise, cultured and virtuous man who would some day turn to God, His Messenger and Islám. He was sadly disappointed at his negligence. The Apostle blessed him and said kind words to him.

Particular events that took place on that memorable Friday, 17 Ramadan AH2 (March 13, 624), the division of the booty, stories of ransoming the captives and the significance of this Battle will be themes of the following chapters.

OUTSTANDING INCIDENTS
AT BADR

A Lesson in Chivalry

As noted earlier, the Prophet ordered his companions at Badr to refrain from killing Abu'l-Bakhtari. Now, al-Mujadhdhar encountered him and told him that the Apostle had forbidden them to kill him. As it happened he had a friend Junada riding with him. "What about my friend here?" he asked. "No, by God." said al-Mujadhdhar, "I cannot spare your friend. My orders are about you only." "In that case," he said, "I will die with him. The women of Makkah shall not say that I forsook my friend to save my own life." Then he recited this verse:

A son of the free betrays not his friend
Till he's dead, or sees him safe on his way.

Both lost their lives in the skirmish that ensued. Al-Mujadhdhar brought the distasteful news to the Apostle and said that he had tried his best to avoid a fight, but that Abu'l-Bakhtari had insisted on fighting with fatal result to himself.

Sweet Revenge

In a previous story we became acquainted with Umayyah b. Khalaf and his slave Bilal, how in the scorching mid-day sun of Arabia he would have him lie on his back, put a heavy stone on his chest and vow that he would not release him until he abandoned the religion of Muhammad, and how Bilal kept saying, 'One! One!' meaning that God is one and he could not declare otherwise. Now in the pell-mell at Badr this same Umayyah was standing holding his son 'Ali's hand when he met an old friend, a Muslim, carrying coats of mail which he had looted. Disgusted with the fighting that was going on around him, he asked this old friend to abandon the loot and take him and his son prisoners as the ransom would be far more valuable than the coats of mail, saying, "I never saw a day like this. Have you no use for milk?"[81] 'Abdu'l-Rahman, for that was the friend's name, readily agreed, threw away the loot and took Umayyah and his son prisoners

As he was walking between the father and the son holding them by the hand and taking them off to where prisoners were kept, who would suddenly espy them but Bilal. "The arch-infidel Umayyah b.Khalaf!" he cried, "May I not live if he lives." "Would you attack my prisoners?" 'Abdu'l-Rahman protested. Bilal's shout rang through the multitude, "O God's Helpers, the arch-infidel Umayyah b.Khalaf! May I not live if he lives!" The Muslims formed a ring around them. 'Abdu'l-Rahman appealed to his prisoners to escape as he found himself unable to rescue them. But escape was impossible. They were both killed and cut into pieces. Abdu'l-Rahman used to say, "God have mercy on Bilal. I lost my coats of mail and he deprived me of my prisoners."

The Fate of Abu Jahl

When the enemy was routed, the Apostle ordered a search to be made among the corpses for Abu Jahl's body, and turning his face to heaven, he said, "O God, don't let him escape Thee!" Mu'adh was the first to spot him in a thicket out of reach. But he was able to get close enough to send a leg of his flying with a blow. 'Ikrima, Abu Jahl's son, struck him a blow which severed his arm. It was hanging by the skin on his side the rest of the day as he went on fighting until it became too painful to bear. He then put the dangling arm under his foot and tore it off. Mu'adh lived nearly twenty years after this incident.

The next blow came from Mu'awwidh's sword leaving him lying helpless in the thicket breathing his last. Then he was

---

[81] The statement hints that he could get milch camels, which would be more valuable than coats of mail.

espied by 'Abdullah b.Masud, who put his foot upon his neck (Abu Jahl "had once clawed at him and punched him at Makkah"), and said, "Has God put you to shame, you enemy of God?" Then he cut off his head and brought it to the Apostle, saying, "This is the head of the enemy of God, Abu Jahl!" He threw the head before the Prophet, who gave thanks to God.

Angels Fought at Badr in Defence of the Muslims

Throughout the day of Badr, the Messenger of God kept on supplicating the Lord for the help He had promised him. "O God, if this band of people perishes today you will not be worshipped after today" he entreated. Time and time again, he would cry out from the depth of his soul. "O God, I ask you to keep your contract and your promise..." Abu Bakr took his hand and said, "This is enough, O Prophet of God. You have tired your Lord with your importuning. God will assuredly fulfil what He has promised you." And God did indeed fulfil His promise as revealed in several verses of the eighth Sura, al-Anfal.

Verse 9　　When ye asked assistance of your Lord, and He answered you, Verily I will assist you with a

Verse 10　Thousand angels, following one another. And this God designed only as good tidings for you, and that your hearts might thereby rest secure, for victory is from God alone; and God is mighty and wise.

Verse 11　When a sleep fell on you, and he sent down upon you water from heaven, that He might confirm your

Verse 12　Hearts, and establish your feet thereby. Also when thy Lord spake unto the angels, Verily I am with you; wherefore confirm those who believe. I will cast a dread into the hearts of the unbelievers.

Therefore strike off their heads, and strike off all the ends of their fingers.

Verse 13   This shall they suffer, because they have resisted God and His Apostle: and whosoever shall oppose God and His Apostle, verily God will be severe in punishing him.

Extraordinary tales have been reported concerning the participation of angels in the Battle of Badr. One said that while he and his cousin, both being polytheists, were standing on top of a hill watching the battle below, waiting for it to end so that they could join in the loot, they heard the neighing of horses and a voice saying "Forward, Hayzum!"[82] The cousin died instantly of fright. He said he would have had the same fate had he not gained control of himself. Another who had fought at Badr and had became blind did not have the slightest doubt of the actual location in the glen where the angels appeared. And yet a third warrior said that he was approaching his prey to blow off his head, when the head fell off without his sword touching it. He was sure an unseen hand had killed him. Some observed that they had seen the angels at Badr with their white turbans flowing behind them. They said that the angels participated in the fighting at Badr only and in no other expedition.

Two of the Prophet's Arch-enemies Killed

On their return journey to Madinah, at al-Safra' Nadr b. al-Harith, one of the satans of Quraysh, was killed by 'Ali at the Apostle's behest. This was the man who throughout the years of Muhammad's stay in Makka after his appointment to Prophethood, had poured on him insults and indignities beyond measure. When the Apostle recited Revelations,

---

[82] The name of Gabriel's horse.

concerning the Messengers of the past, he announced publicly that they were the stories of the ancients, and that the story of Rustam and Isfandiyar, which he had picked up in his travels, were more interesting and enlightening and that in story-telling he was decidedly better talented than Muhammad.

At the next station, 'Uqba received a similar fate. His story has been mentioned here before. He once spat on the Apostle's face only to please a bosom friend[83].

---

[83] Blessed is the man that hath acknowledged his belief in God and in His signs, and recognized that "He shall not be asked of His doings". Such a recognition has been made by God the ornament of every belief and its very foundation. Upon it must depend the acceptance of every goodly deed. Fasten your eyes upon it, that haply the whisperings of the rebellious may not cause you to slip. Were He to decree as lawful the thing which from time immemorial had been forbidden, and forbid that which had, at all times, been regarded as lawful, to none is given the right to question His authority. Whoso will hesitate, though it be for less than a moment, should be regarded as a transgressor.

Bahá'u'lláh

'The Kitáb-i-Aqdas' # 161, 162, p. 77 "... The purport is this that the Holy Manifestations of God do as They wish and ordain that which They Please. Whatsoever They bid should be obeyed; doubts and suspicions as to whether a command appears to be in conformity with justice and equity should in no way be entertained. This mental perplexity will end in sedition and grievous corruption..."

'Abdu' l-Bahá, cited in *Ma'idiy-i-Asmani*, vol. 2, pp. 42/3 (Author's translation)

THE BATTLE OF BADR: THE DIVISION OF THE BOOTY

Dispute over the spoils arose among the Muslims. Those in possession of the booty claimed it as their own, as was the custom among the Arabs. Those who engaged the enemy but had not been able to come into the possession of any property claimed that their efforts deserved recognition and had it not been for them their fellow Muslims could not have gotten anything. And then there were those who acted as the Prophet's bodyguards at his command post, built of palm branches, and who had no active part in the fighting but maintained that their role in protecting the Apostle from enemy attack was important and therefore claimed equal share in the booty.

The Sura al-Anfal (the 8th Sura) was revealed concerning the battle of Badr. It opens by stating that the spoils are God's and the Apostle's and lays down the duty of a believer to have faith in and to fear God, and to obey His Messenger; it reminds them that they desired the Caravan and worldly gain, but God purposed to defeat the party of Quraysh to 'verify the truth, and destroy falsehood' 'that God might accomplish the thing which was decreed to be done' It recalls God's assistance to them with a thousand angels, in causing rain to fall, and casting dread in the hearts of their enemies; it encourages the believers to battle falsehood with their heart and soul, never turning back, 'but persevere with patience, for God is with those who persevere'; it admonishes the believers to beware sedition which affects the whole community, to be loyal to God and His Apostle; it warns against worldliness 'Ye seek the accidental goods of this world, but God desires the life to come'; it justifies God's severe punishment of the unbelievers for their ungodly conduct in persecuting the believers and obstructing the way of God; it assures the ungodly of the mercy of God to the sincere penitent but urges the believer to fight against idolatry until 'the religion be wholly God's'; it inspires them to be prepared with all resources necessary to 'strike terror into the enemy of God', and promises compensation for all they expend in the defence of religion but declares that 'if they incline unto peace, do thou also incline thereto'; it asserts that love and unity between hearts cannot be achieved by the expenditure of wealth and riches, but by faith in God's will and purpose; and it reveals ordinances concerning (a) the division of the spoils, (b) 'a fifth part thereof belongeth to God, and to the Apostle, and his kindred, and the orphans, and the poor, and the traveller', (c) the establishment of kinship between the Emigrants and the Helpers, (d) believers who did not emigrate to Madinah have no claim to kinship until they emigrate, (e) and the infidels are kins the one to the other, but not to any of the believers.

Now the Prophet ordered the booty be collected in one place, and put 'Abdullah b.Ka'b in charge of it. At al-Naziya, He divided it equally among the Muslims who participated in the expedition of Badr. He gave a few items to persons who specifically desired and solicited them. Then he returned to Madinah.

STORIES RELATED TO THE RANSOMING OF SOME CAPTIVES

Word went around in Makkah asking the Quraysh not to bewail their dead lest the Muslims rejoice over their misfortune, and not to be in a hurry to seek freedom of prisoners so that excessive ransoms may not be demanded. But some, while outwardly agreeing that to hurry in this affair was to their detriment, slipped away at night to redeem the captives.

Some of these captives were closely related to the Prophet. Their stories, therefore, are of spacial interest.

The Story of Al-'Abbas

Al-Abbas was the Prophet's uncle. His wife Umm'l-Fadl and some of his slaves accepted Islám soon after Muhammad raised his call. 'Abbas, however, was wavering. He resented hostility with his own people, so he concealed his faith. Now he was a hefty man and his captor Abu'l-Yasar was a little man. The Apostle wondered how he could have captured him. "A man I had never seen before or after helped me," he said, and he described him. The Prophet said, "A noble angel helped you against him." It is said that on the night of Badr, the Messenger of God was restless. His companions were worried. "I hear the writhing of al-'Abbas in prison," he explained. So they set him free and the Apostle slept soundly thereafter.

Abu Bakr and 'Umar disagreed over what to do with al-'Abbas. Abu Bakr believed they should release him without a ransom as he was the Prophet's uncle. 'Umar was of the opinion that he be shown no mercy and that his head should be cut off. When he was brought to the Prophet in Madinah, he asked him to pay ransom for himself, as well as for his two nephews 'Aqil, ('Alí's brother) and Naufal, and for an ally 'Utba, as he was a rich man. "I was a Muslim," said 'Abbas, "and came to Badr under compulsion." "God knows best about your Islám," replied Muhammad. "If what you say is true, God will reward you for it: Now the Apostle had taken twenty okes of gold from him. "O Apostle of God, credit me with them in my ransom," he requested. "That has nothing to do with it," answered the Prophet. "God took that from you and gave it to us," 'Abbas said, "I have no money." "Then where is the money which you left with Ummu'l-Fadl when you left Makkah? You two were alone when you said to her, "If I am killed so much is for al-Fadl, 'Abdullah, and Qutham and 'Ubaydullah'." "By Him Who sent you with the truth," 'Abbas exclaimed, "none but she and I knew of this and now I know that you are God's Apostle." So, he paid up the ransom for himself and the afore-mentioned three men. It gladdened the Apostle's heart to see that his uncle was confirmed in his faith in God.

The Story of Zaynab and her Husband

Zaynab was the Apostle's daughter. Her husband was Abu'l'As a worthy merchant and of the nobility of Makkah. To spite the Prophet, while still in Makkah the Quraysh offered him any woman he desired if only he would divorce Zaynab and send her packing, but he refused to do so. Abu'l'As now became a prisoner in Madinah. Zaynab sent the ransom money together with a necklace given to her by her mother on her wedding day. The Prophet was greatly touched and, overcome by feelings of sympathy and affection, said to the believers, "If you would like to let her have her captive husband back and return her money to her, do so." The believers obeyed. He was released, and the money was retruned.

Abu'l'As returned to Makkah and asked Zaynab to rejoin her father. Her journey to Madinah was quite an adventure. The Quraysh would not let her leave the city in broad daylight. Her brother-in-law who was escorting her tried to defend her, but was overpowered. She had to return home and stay a few days until the hubbub settled. And then in the thick of night she was conducted out of the city and handed over to the Prophet's emissary who had been sent by him to wait for her at a place outside Makkah and accompany her to Madinah.

After that Zaynab and her husband were separated for several years. She lived with her father in Madinah; he continued his business in Makkah until shortly before the conquest of Makkah. He was retuning home from Syria with much merchandise when he was attacked by a raiding party that plundered everything he had. He himself escaped and sought Zaynab's protection. At the morning prayer in the mosque the following day, Zaynab announced in a loud voice from the women's side, "O you men, I have given protection to Abu'l'As." The Prophet confessed to the men after the prayer that he had known nothing about her declaration, adding, "The meanest Muslim can give protection on their behalf." He then told Zaynab that she should honour her guest but should not allow him to approach her as she was not lawful to him[84]. He also sent word to the raiding party telling them that Abu'l'As was his son-in-law and that, though the booty was theirs by right and they could dispose of it as they wished, he would be pleased it they saw fit to restore it to him. They returned every last bit of the loot.

Abu'l'As then went to Makkah and paid the people, who had entrusted him with money, their due. When he made sure that they were no further claims on him and that the people were totally satisfied and grateful to him he said, "Then I bear witness that there is no god but God and that Muhammad is His servant and His Messenger. I would have become a Muslim when I was with him but that I feared that you would think that I only wanted to rob you of your property; and now that God has restored it to you and I am clear of it I submit myself to God." He rejoined the Apostle and Zaynab, his loving wife.

---

[84] "... and marry not idolaters until they believe. A believing slave is preferred to an idolater even though he pleases you (more)." 2:221

SIGNIFICANCE OF THE BATTLE
OF BADR

The victory of the Muslims at Badr was not the triumph of an Arab tribe over another. It was the conquest of Islám consisting of a body of believers from a wide range of clans affiliated with different tribes. This had profound implications. The age-old tribal tie of kinship was forever destroyed and the brotherhood of Islám succeeded it. The kinship of the believers one with the other, regardless to what tribe they belonged, as against the mutual kinship of the unbelievers, was introduced. And as more and more tribes entered under the banner of Islám, the unity of Arabia under one common Faith became a reality. God's Revelation concerning this is quite clear:

> And hath made their hearts one. Hadst thou spent all there is in the earth, thou couldst not have united their hearts; but God hath united them, for He is Mighty, Wise.
>
> Q. 8: 63

> Verily, they who have believed and fled their homes and have striven for the Cause of God with their substance and their selves and they who have given shelter and rendered help, shall be nearest of kin the one to the other. But they who have believed, but have not fled their country, ye are not responsible for their protection until they flee... And as to the unbelievers, they are kin the one to the other. Unless ye do this, there will be sedition in the land and grievous corruption.
>
> Q. 8: 72, 73

A second important effect of the victory at Badr was the selfesteem it generated in the hearts of the believers. During the years in Makkah the Prophet had warned and threatened divine visitations, but patiently bore humiliation and persecution. The believers, too, accepted persecution with resignation and the hope of ultimate victory as God promised. Now, for the first time, they experienced the fulfilment of that promise especially as they were outnumbered three to one. They were in poor spirits so far, now they stood tall and were accounted heroes. When a Muslim congratulated them on their way back from Badr, one of them said, "What are you congratulating us about? By God, we only met some bald old women like the sacrificial camels who are hobbled, and we slaughtered them!" Whereupon the Prophet, overhearing him, remarked, "But, nephew, those were the chiefs." And indeed the main body of the chiefs and leaders of the Quray<u>sh</u> fell on the battleground of Badr.

And they were even more heartened by God's words that were recited to them:

And think not that the unbelievers shall escape Us. They shall not weaken God. Make ready then against them what force ye can and troops of horse, whereby ye may strike terror into the enemy of God and your enemy, and into others beside them whom ye know not, but whom God knoweth. All that you shall expend for the Cause of God shall be repaid you; and ye shall not be wronged. And if they lean to peace, lean thou also to it; and put thy trust in God: for He is the Hearing, the Knowing. But if they seek to betray thee, God will be all-sufficient for thee. It is He Who hath strengthened thee with His help, and with the faithful.

                                                      Q. 8: 59-62

The unexpected defeat of the mightiest tribe of Arabia brought dignity to the Messenger of God in the sight of non-Muslims and raised the status of Islám, hitherto the object of ridicule and derision among the tribes. This led to a sudden surge of conversion both on a personal level and on a tribal plane. The tribes gradually approached the Prophet with respect and began to recognize his claim to be the Messenger of God and the voice of truth.

The Revelation of the Sura al-Anfal was another important consequence of Badr. The contents of this Sura have been discussed in previous sections. Apart from its value as a document containing legislation, it has a number of moral and spiritual concepts well deserving serious relection.

THE CONVERSION OF 'UMAYR B. WAHB

'Umayr was a chief of Quray<u>sh</u> who fought at Badr together with his son. He was spared and returned to Makkah. His son was among the prisoners that were taken to Madinah. Like most of the Quray<u>sh</u> chiefs, 'Umayr had caused the Prophet and his companions much pain and distress in Makkah. He also saw the corpses of his peers being thrown into the pit at Badr in shame and disgrace. One day, shortly after his return to Makkah, he was sitting chatting with Safwan, an old friend. Safwan said, "By God, there is no good in life now they are dead." 'Umayr filled with rage agreed and said, "Were it not for a debt outstanding against me and a family I cannot afford to leave unprovided for, I would ride to Madinah and kill Muhammad, for I have good cause against the lot of them, my son being a prisoner in their hands." Safwan agreed to pay his debt and take care of his family if he undertook the task. They agreed to keep the matter secret.

'Umayr prepared for the journey, sharpened his sword, rubbed poison on the blade and set out for Madinah. 'Umar saw him standing at the door of the mosque wearing his sword and had no misgiving about his intention. He reported the matter to the Prophet. He said, "Bring him in to me." 'Umayr greeted the Messenger of God with the customary "Good morning." The Apostle replied with the Muslim salutation "al-Salam" meaning "peace" and said, "This is the greeting of the people of Paradise." "By God, Muhammad," he said, "You have not been using this expression for long." "What brought you here?" asked the Prophet. "I have come about this prisoner you have that you may treat him well." "Then why have you a sword round your neck?" "God damn the swords. Have they done us any good?" "Tell me the truth. Why have you come?" "I came only for the reason I have told you." The Prophet then told him word for word the conversation he had had with Safwan while they sat in the hijr lamenting over the dead of Quray<u>sh</u> buried in the well, and how he agreed to pay 'Umayr's debt and take care of his family on condition that he would kill the Apostle. Stunned at the revelation of a discussion known only to him and Safwan, he knelt before the Apostle and said, "I testify that you are the Messenger of God. We used to call you a liar when you brought us tidings from heaven and we denied the revelation you brought. But this is a matter to which only I and Safwan were privy, and none can have told you of it but God. Praise be to God Who has guided me to Islám and led me thus." The Apostle said to the Muslims present to instruct 'Umayr in the Faith and teach him to recite and understand the Qur'án, and to set his captive free. And so it was done.

'Umayr asked the Prophet's permission to return to Makkah and teach the Faith to the Makkans. "Perhaps God will guide them to the truth; but if they persist in rebellion and denial, I will persecute them as I persecuted your companions." The Messenger of God gave him permission.'Umayr called the Makkans to God and His Apostle and through his teaching effort many became Muslims.

THE EXPULSION OF THE B. QAYNUQA'

The three Jewish tribes that lived each in its separate quarter in close proximity to Madinah did not observe the terms of their compact with the Messenger of God with honesty and good faith. They considered the Prophet's victory at Badr a threat to their very existence. Instead of taking a conciliatory attitude towards him, they challenged him hoping to exterminate his Cause. When God revealed in the Sura al-Anfal:

> And if thou fear treachery from any people, violate their contract in like manner, for God loveth not the treacherous.

Q. 8: 58

the Messenger of God said, "I fear the Banu Qaynuqa." He had them assembled in their market-place and addressed them as follows: O Jews, beware lest God bring upon you the vengeance that He brought upon Quray<u>sh</u>, and become Muslims. You know that I am a Prophet sent by God. You will find that in your Scriptures and in God's covenant with you." They replied, "O Muhammad, you seem to think that we are your people. Do not deceive yourself because you encountered a people with no knowledge of war and got the better of them; for by God, if we fight you, you will find that we are real men!" No challenge could be more explicit. The Apostle received a fresh Revelation:

> Say unto those who believe not: Ye shall be overcome and gathered together into Hell; and wretched the couch! Ye have already had a sign in the meeting of

---

[85] at Badr.

the two hosts[85]. The one host fought in the Cause of God, and the other were infidels. To their own eyesight, the infidels saw you twice as many as themselves. And God strengtheneth with His help whom He pleaseth. Surely herein was a lesson for men of discernment.

Q. 3: 12-13

They turned deaf ears to his warnings. The Messenger of God besieged them for two weeks. They surrendered. 'Abdullah b. Ubayy, the leader of the Munafiqin (the Hypocrites), went to the Prophet and said, "O Muhammad, deal kindly with my clients[86]. "He was very rough with the Prophet, took Him by the collar and would not let him go until he said, "You can have them."

'Ubadah of the Banu-'Auf who had the same alliance with the Jews renounced all responsibility for them in favour of the Apostle, saying, "O Apostle of God. I take God and His Apostle and the believers as my friends, and I renounce my agreement and friendship with these unbelievers." The following passage was revealed concerning this matter:

O Believers! take not the Jews or Christians as friends. They are but one another's friends. If any one of you taketh them for his friends, he surely is one of them! God will not guide the evil-doers. So shalt thou see the deseased at heart[87] speed away to them and say, "We fear lest a change of fortune befall us..."

Q. 5: 51, 52

The Banu Qaynuqa' was expelled. They had no landed property. They were goldsmiths. Their weapons and tools of trade were confiscated.

---

[86] The Banu Qaynuqa' had an alliance with the Khazraj before Muhammad came to Madinah.

[87] Ref. to 'Abdullah b. Ubayy

THE STORY OF KA'B B. AL-ASHRAF

Ka'b b. al-Ashraf was a half-breed from an Arab father and a Jewish mother. He was a very wealthy man who lived in his own stronghold in the southern section of Madinah. His hostility to the Apostle of God was public knowledge. He incited the people against him, composed satiric verses ridiculing him and did everything to insult and humiliate him. When news of the defeat of Quraysh and the decimation of their chiefs reached him, he said, "Could this be really true? Can Muhammad have killed these people who were nobles of the Arabs and the kings of men? If this be true, then the belly of the earth is a better place for us than its surface!"

Ka'b then left for Makkah and inflamed the Quraysh against the Apostle, reciting verses, bewailing the Quraysh buried in the well. Sale relates from Al-Baydawi and Jalal-al-Din Suyuti and others that "Ka'b ibn al-Ashraf, with forty horses went and made a league with Abu Sufyan, which they confirmed by oath." (The Koran Sura 59: 2 fn. 2.) And when he returned to Madinah, he composed insulting love poems on some Muslim women. Such conduct jeopardized the tranquility of the community in Madinah. The Prophet's patience was wearing thin by such Jewish elements who treacherously stabbed him in the back. He said to the Muslims present with him one day, "Who will rid me of Ka'b?" Muhammad b.Maslama volunteered, on condition that the Prophet would permit him to resort to lies and trickery if need be. The Prophet said, "Say what you like, for you are free in the matter." He found four other Muslims who agreed to undertake the task with him, one of whom was known as Abu Na'ila who occasionally visited Ka'b to recite poetry to each other. The five agreed on a plot.

Na'ila visited Ka'b, and in the course of conversation complained about life in Madinah after Muhammad's arrival in the city. "What with the hostility of the Bedouins resulting in roads being unsafe for travel, and families having to support the 'Emigrants', everybody is indeed suffering, " he said. "Didn't I, Ibn al-Ashraf, warn you, Ibn Salamah, that things would turn out like this?" said Ka'b. Na'ila slowly and tactfully turned to a new subject. "I would like you," he said "to sell us some food. We will give you a surety and make a firm contract. But please treat us generously." "Give me your sons as a pledge," said Ka'b. "You wish to insult us. I have friends who also wish to buy food, and we are ready to deposit weapons and coats of mail, but please deal with us generously in this matter. Ka'b considered weapons a good pledge. Then Na'ilah left, joined his companions and related to them what had happened, and asked them to arm themselves. They all went then to meet the Apostle.

It is said that the Prophet walked with them a distance, then sent them off, saying, "Go in God's name; O God help them!" It was a moonlit night. When they reached Ka'b's castle, Na'ila called out to him. He had only recently married, and had gone to bed. He recognized Na'ila's voice and jumped out of bed. His wife had a premonition of danger and said, "By God, I can feel evil in his voice." Ka'b answered, "It is Abu Na'ila. But even if the call were for a stab a brave man must answer it." So saying, he put on a cloak and went down to talk to them. The fact that they were all armed to the hilt did not worry him since they had promised him weapons and coats of mail as their pledge. They talked for a while. Na'ila suggested they should walk to Shi'b al-'Ajuz so that they can finalize the deal. "If you like," answered Ka'b and they all walked together distancing themselves from the castle. When they had gone far enough, they suddenly attacked him. "Smite the enemy of God!" shouted Na'ilah. Swords flashed in the moonlit night and blows came down hard with but little effect. Ka'b's cries awakened the neighbourhood and lamps were lit in several houses. Muhammad b. Maslama remembered he was carrying a sharp dagger in his scabbard. He thrust it into Ka'b's body and pressed it down to his genitals. Ka'b stopped crying and fell. One of the five was accidentally smitten by a sword and was bleeding. He could not move fast. They waited for him in a safe place after having passed through inhabited quarters. He joined them and they carried him to the Prophet at the end of the night. He was standing in prayer. When he finished, they greeted him and gave him the news of Ka'b's death. He spat on their friend's wound, and he and they returned home. Their exploit cast terror among the Jews; and there was not a Jew but feared for his life.

THE BATTLE OF UHUD

After the defeat at Badr and the loss of a great number of their nobles and leaders, Abu Sufyan arrived in Makkah with the Caravan followed by the routed escapes from Badr. The Quraysh had never been so humbled before, and vowed revenge. The normal trade route to Syria was at risk as long as the Muslims had power in Madinah. Meanwhile the Quraysh could not stay inactive in Makkah since they would soon consume their capital. They decided to man a caravan and send it north on the Najd road. They hired an expert guide, named Furat, and the caravan set out. When the Prophet learned of this affair, he mounted an expedition to intercept the caravan. Taken by surprise, the men leading the caravan escaped, leaving behind a rich booty of silver and merchandise. It is said that the share of the Prophet amounted to twenty thousand dirhams of silver. The other four fifths was then distributed among the members of the expedition. Furat, the only captive, accepted Islám and was set free.

Abu Sufyan was enraged and swore he would abstain from sexual intercourse until he had raided Muhammad. He equipped two hundred riders and took the Najd road towards Madinah. A short distance from Madinah, they encamped. Abu Sufyan then hurried forth under cover of darkness to the quarters of Banu al-Nadir. One or two of the Jews were affraid of him and did not open their doors to him. Sallam, then chief of the tribe, however, took him in, gave him food and drink and provided all the information he had about the Muslims. It was still dark when Abu Sufyan rejoined his men. He sent a few of them to Madinah. These men burned some young palm trees and killed a couple of Madinans who were working in the fields. But people were warned and the Apostle and some companions went in pursuit. The raiders eluded them, but they were able to collect bags of provision which they had thrown away to lighten their burden so as to get away quickly.

The reader can now get a good picture of the plight of the Makkan Quraysh and the stranglehold the Muslims had upon their adversaries. Meanwhile satirists and poets like Ka'b ibn al-Ashraf fanned the flame of rage in their hearts. And the sons, brothers and cousins, of the nobles killed at Badr fumed with revenge and urged upon the wealthy Quraysh the need to gather money to fight Muhammad, whom they considered to be the root cause of their suffering, hoping to avenge their lost ones. Had not God anticipated their thoughts in the Sura al-Anfal?

They who believe not, expend their wealth to obstruct the way of God: they shall expend it, but afterwards it shall be to them sighing and regret, and at length they shall be overcome: and the unbelievers shall be gathered together unto hell.

Q. 8: 36

So the Quraysh contributed the gains they had acquired from Abu Sufyan's Caravan towards the equipment of troops and preparation of a force of 3000 men, of whom 700 were armed with coats of mail, and 200 horses. The Banu Kinanah allied themselves with the Quraysh. Fifteen women of repute including Hind d. 'Utba, wife of Abu Sufyan, accompanied the troops with their tambourines, singing songs and inciting the men to avenge the fallen at Badr.

Hind sang:

O ye sons of 'Abdu'l-Dar,
O ye protectors of our rear,
Smite with every sharpened spear!

and:

If you advance we hug you,
Spread soft rugs beneath you;

> If you retreat we leave you,
> Leave and no more love you.

Thus the Makkan army advanced and took positions at Uhud, a mountain some four miles to the North of Madinah, and remained there Wednesday to Friday. The battle took place on Saturday, March 23, 625 A.D.

When the Apostle heard that the Quraysh had camped at Uhud, he agreed with 'Abdullah ibn Ubayy[88] that the city offered the best defensive position against enemy attack. But the majority of the Muslims said, "O Messenger of God, lead us out to our enemies so that they may not think that we are too cowardly and weak to face them." 'Abdullah begged Muhammad not to heed them, but to follow his advice and remain in Madinah. He reminded him that in the past whenever they went out to meet the enemy they suffered losses. He said that if the Quraysh attack us even our women and children would be able to hurl stones at them and they would withdraw disappointed. In the end the Apostle was persuaded to face the enemy in the battlefield. The Muslim army consisted of a thousand men, of whom one hundred wore coats of mail. They had only two horses, one belonging to the Prophet, the other to a Muslim. There were also fifty archers. They left Madinah on Friday after the mid-day prayer. Midway to Uhud 'Abdullah decided to split and told his men, "He (meaning the Prophet) obeyed them by setting out and disobeyed me. By God, we do not know why we should get ourselves killed here, men." So he withdrew with three hundred of his men to Madinah, reducing the Muslim force to seven hundred. When some of the Muslims importuned

---

[88] 'Abdullah was the leader of the band of Hypocrites. Outwardly, he professed Islám but in reality he was the Prophet's enemy. 'Abdullah was an ambitious man who wanted leadership in Madinah and considered the Prophet a stumbling block to achieving this ambition. His desire to join forces with the Muslims was prompted by material gain for booty.

him not to desert, he replied, "If we knew what we were going to fight, we would not desert you, but we do not think that there is going to be a battle."

The Prophet positioned his men, some under al-Zubayr had orders to engage the cavalry, some under Hamzih marched out at the head of the men who had no armour. The archers were under the command of 'Abdullah ibn Jubayr and were ordered to "defend us against the cavalry with your arrows, and do not leave your position, if you see us victorious, and if you see them victorious, do not come to our assistance. When the battle started, the Muslims fought bravely, Hamzih and 'Alí displayed exceptional bravery, dispersing groups of the Quray<u>sh</u>, who were soon put to rout. The women, shrieking, pulled up their skirts and flew in different directions. The archers, greedy after loot, raised the cry "Booty! Booty!" and rushed forth, chasing the fleeing enemy. The voices of 'Abdullah and a few of the archers warning them of the Apostle's orders not to abandon their position under any circumstances fell on deaf ears. The right wing of the enemy cavalry commanded by Khalid ibn al-Walid, now attacked from the rear and turned the table on the Muslims who suffered heavily losing seventy dead and many wounded. The Apostle of God received wounds on his cheeks and forehead. Two of his lower incisors were broken and his lip was split. At one point, someone shouted, "The Messenger of God has been killed." Friends and foes looked at each other in consternation and disbelief. It was, indeed a distressful day.

Now Jubayr had an Abyssinian slave named Wahshi, nick-named Abu Dasmah, who was skilful at throwing a javelin and rarely missed his target. He had promised to set him free if he killed Hamzih[89], the Prophet's uncle, in revenge for his own uncle who had fallen at Badr. Every time Hind passed

---

[89] The Apostle used to call him "The Lion of God," Bahá'u'lláh called him "The Prince of Martyrs." See Iqán, p. 121.

by Wahshi, she would say, "Go to it, Abu Dasmah! Quench my thirst for vengeance, and quench your own!" or, "Come on, you father of blackness, satisfy your vengeance and ours!" For at Badr Hamzih had killed Hind's father, too. While Hamzih was hurling blows left and right, killing the enemy with his sword Wahshi took aim and launched his javelin at him. It pierced his body and he collapsed. Hind and some other of the women folk then mutilated the corpses of the Muslims, cutting off their noses and ears. Hind made them into anklets and collars and presented these to Wahshi. She cut out Hamzih's liver and chewed it, but, unable to swallow it, she threw it away.

By the end of the day the combatants were exhausted. The dead of the Muslims were seventy, the same number of the dead of Quraysh at Badr. Twenty-two of the Quraysh fell in the field that day. Abu Sufyan talked to the Quraysh, praising their valour. "The victory today in exchange for the day of Badr," he said, 'Umar then got up at the behest of the Apostle and said, "God is most High and most Glorious! We are not equal. Our dead are in Paradise; your dead in Hell." Abu Sufyan then asked 'Umar whether it was true that Muhammad was dead as Ibn Qami'a claimed. "By God, Ibn Qami'a lies! The Apostle is listening to what you are saying now," 'Umar replied. When Abu Sufyan and his compatriots were leaving, he called out, "Your meeting place in Badr next year." The Apostle ordered one to reply, "Yes, it is an appointment between us."

It is still unclear for historians why the Quraysh did not follow up on their victory. What caused their retreat is still uncertain. A couple of days after they left Uhud, they themselves questioned their failure to pursue the Muslims, and suggestion was made that they should return to complete their victory, but most had no stomach for fighting.

The Muslims searched for their dead and wounded. The Apostle went in search of Hamzih. Relatives of the dead came from Madinah. Some had taken their dead to Madinah and buried them there. The Apostle forbade this. The dead were buried in the valley, two and sometimes three sharing a grave, and prayers were read for them.

In the third Sura of the Qur'án, "The Family of 'Imrán," Verses 121-129 and 139 -175 refer to the battle of Uhud, and the main incidents are highlighted there.

THE EXPULSION OF BANU AL-NADIR

It was the characteristic of the Arab tribes to resort to treachery and deception in their dealings with one another, either for material gains or for assertion of power. This led to feuds, bloodshed, and revenge. Two instances of treachery occured after the battle of Uhud.

Some members of a tribe that professed Islám, asked the Apostle to send teachers to their tribe to recite the Qur'án to them and to teach them the ordinances of the Faith. A delegation of six or ten, opinions vary, were dispatched. When they reached al-Raji', a watering place of Hudhayl somewhere between Makkah and Taif, the men betrayed the Muslim teachers. Bedouines from the tribe of Hudhayl surrounded them and swore by God that they would but kill them but that they would sell them to the Makkans to make some money. The Muslims, thereupon, defended themselves and all, but two who surrendered, were killed. The two were bought in Makkah and put to death to avenge the killing of relatives at Uhud.[90]

---

[90] In a Tablet addressed to 'Andalib, addressing Himself to the issue that in all ages people of negation have protested against the judgments and utterances of the Messengers of God, Baháu'lláh cites events in the Ministry of Muhammad to illustrate His point. The above incident is related thus: "Salaqih, whose husband and sons had been killed in the battle of Uhud, said to Sufyan that she would give one hundred camels to anyone who would kill their murderers. The fire of greed and avarice was ablaze in Sufyan's heart. He dispatched seven Arabs to Madinah who would feign faith in Islám and allegiance to the Prophet, and would ask Him to send a few of the companions to teach the permissible and the forbidden ordinances of Islám. The Apostle of God chose ten of His companions, including 'Asim and ordered them to go with the seven and teach the tribes the precepts of Islám. This they proceeded to do forthwith. When they reached their destination there occurred what was the cause of great grief to the people of Madinah. Some of the hypocrites greatly rejoicing their misfortune, sarcastically remarked: 'And why didn't Muhammad's God inform Him that they were dissemblers?' They then pronounced the judgment of ignorance and lack of knowledge upon him." Iqtidarat, p. 7.

The second incident took place in Bi'r Ma'una. Abu Bara' 'Amir, chief of the Banu 'Amir, presented the Apostle with a gift. He said that He could accept it only if he became a Muslim. They had a long conversation, and the Qur'án was recited to him, but he did not accept Islám. He was so fascinated, however, that he asked the Apostle to send teachers to his tribe, and guaranteed protection for them, noticing that the Prophet had doubts about their safety. A delegation to forty, or seventy, accounts vary, was sent forthwith. The party encamped at Bi'r Ma'una. One was sent with the Apostle's letter to 'Amir, the nephew of Abu 'Amir, who was then in the position of leadership there, informing him of the purpose of the delegation and the pact of protection given them. Without reading the letter, he killed the emissary. His own tribesmen refused to fight the Muslims saying that Abu 'Amir had given them protection, but a few clans of Banu Sulaym agreed to assist him. They surrounded their camp and killed all, but one who was badly wounded and was given up for dead. Two Muslims grazing camels at a distance noticed vultures hovering in the sky, and went to see what had happened. They found the Muslims lying in their blood and the horsemen watching them. One of them ran towards Madinah to inform the Messenger of God. On his way, he met two men of the 'Amir tribe. He waited until they fell asleep, rushed and killed them, not aware that these two were under the Apostle's protection.

Now when the Prophet was asked to pay blood money, He went to the Banu al-Nadir to ask their help for the payment of the blood money. They agreed to this. Then they consulted together privately and, seeing the Prophet resting by a wall of one of their houses, said, "We shall never have such an opportunity again. Let one drop a stone on him from the roof and kill him." 'Amr ibn Jihash volunteered to do so. The Prophet received an intimation of their design from God, suddenly got up and, leaving his companions, 'Alí, Abu Bakr and 'Umar behind, returned straight to Madinah. He told the

Muslims of the treachery intended by the Jews, and called them to prepare for battle.

The three companions of the Prophet returned to Madinah, after waiting for him for some time, and found him sitting in the mosque. He said to them, "The Jews intended to kill me, and God informed me of it." He then sent Muhammad ibn Maslamah to the Jewish tribe with this message: "Leave my country and do not live with me. You have intended treachery." The Jews were astonished that a man of al-Aws, a tribe with whom they had had long association and pacts of friendship, should carry such a message. "Hearts have changed," he replied, "and Islám has wiped out the old covenants." They agreed to leave.

'Abdullah ibn Ubayy, the Hypocrite, sent the Banu al-Nadir a message that they should not leave since he was prepared to assist them with two thousand of his own men. Furthermore, he said, "the Banu Qurayza will also enter battle on your side." When the Banu Qurayza heard of this, they made it known that not one of their men would break his Covenant with Muhammad. Sallam advised Huyayy ibn Akhtab to accept Muhammad's proposal before things would get worse. "What is worse than that?" asked Huyayy. "The seizure of our wealth, the enslavement of our children, and the killing of our fighting men," he replied. Huyayy, however, did not heed his advice and sent a messenger to the Apostle to say: "We will not leave our settlements; so do what you see fit." "Alláh-u-Akbar," said the Apostle. The Muslims echoed. "The Jews have declared war," He announced, and the Prophet's crier invited the Muslims to arm. 'Abdullah ibn Ubayy's son, who was a devoted Muslim, responded to the call and was leaving his house as Huyayy's emissary entered it. 'Abdullah's offer of help proved, alas to be an empty promise. The Jews said, "This is a clever trick of Muhammad."

The Banu Nadir were besieged for fifteen days. They sought peace in utter despair and helplessness, and were now forced to accept harsher terms. They were expelled to Syria; their lands and palm groves were confiscated; every three of them was allowed a camel and a water-skin; except for their coats of mail and weapons, they could carry as much of their movable belongings as their camels could haul. Their lands were divided among the 'Emigrants' and three of the Ansar who were truly poor. Two of the Jews accepted Islám and retained their lands and properties.

"GOD INFORMED ME; GOD WILL PROTECT ME"

In the last chapter we were told that God informed Muhammad of the treacherous design of the Banu Nadir to kill him.

Some may attribute this experience to a hunch, a premonition of approaching danger that is within the experience of all of us. In the lives of the Messengers of God, however, such experiences go beyond a mere feeling of some danger drawing near. If God be unable to protect His Messenger until his task in this world is accomplished, who will? The strong, the wealthy, the political and religious leaders exert a concerted effort to oppose and crush Him and his Cause. He has no support, but God, and in Him he fully and unwaveringly trusts. Two or three other stories in the Apostle's life will perhaps, demonstrate this reality.

The story goes that Abu Jahl, reciting the charges against the Apostle, to the assembly of the nobles of Quraysh in Makkah one day, said to them, "I call God to witness that I will wait for him tomorrow with a heavy stone and when he prostrates himself in prayer I will split his skull with it. Betray me or defend me, let the Banu 'Abd-Manaf[91] do what they like after that." The nobles were most encouraging, and supportive, and promised they would not betray him. The next morning, fully determined to carry out the promised project, Abu Jahl, armed with a heavy stone waited in the Mosque for the Messenger of God. The Prophet came and stood in prayer in the corner of the Mosque, facing Jerusalem, in his usual manner. When he prostrated, Abu Jahl took up the stone and approached him. The nobles of Quraysh sat in a distance awaiting the outcome of Abu Jahl's action.

---

[91] The relatives of Muhammad who protected him.

Suddennly, he was seized with terror, his face was ashen; his knees shook, and the stone fell off his withered hands. The nobles asked him what had happened. He replied, "When I got near him a camel's stallion got in my way. Its head, shoulders and teeth were frightening. It came as though it would eat me." When the Apostle heard this, he said, "That was Gabriel. If Abu Jahl had come nearer, he would have seized him."

Our next story happened years later in Madinah. In a raid in Najd, the Apostle encountered a large force of the Ghatafan tribe. Both sides were afraid that fighting would cause many casualties, and avoided a battle. But one Ghaurath, a member of a clan of Ghatafan said to his people, "Shall I kill Muhammad for you?" "How are you going to manage that?" they asked. He replied that he would take him by surprise. Well, he came to the Apostle and found him sitting with his sword in his lap. "Would you let me look at your sword?" he asked the Apostle. He gave him his sword. The man unsheathed it, and then brandished it, intending to strike him. "Aren't you afraid of me, Muhammad, when I have a sword in my hand?" he asked. "Why should I be afraid of you, when God will protect me?" replied the Messenger of God. Such terror seized the man that he sheathed the sword and returned it to the Apostle.[92]

Some commentators believe that the following passage in the Qur'án was revealed concerning this incident:

"O true believers! Remember God's favour towards you, when certain men designed to stretch forth their hands against you, but he restrained their hands from you; therefore fear God, and in God let the faithful trust."

Q. 5: 11

---

[92] These incidents remind one of a similar incident that happened centuries later in Baghdád when Bahá'u'lláh was visiting a bath and Rida Turk, commissioned by the Persian consul to murder Him, went there, but was so overawed in His presence that he turned on his heel and fled. Read the full account in *'Bahá'u'lláh the King of Glory,'* p. 137

THE BATTLE OF THE DITCH

Do you remember the name Huyayy ibn Akhtab? He was one of the leaders of the Banu Nadir, a mischief-maker who, with a party of his Jewish companions, pledged to fight the Prophet until he was totally destroyed. They went to Makkah and promised to join them in their battle against the Muslims. When asked by the Quraysh whether their idolatrous practices were not better than Muhammad's religion, the Jews assured them that they were better guided than the Muslims. God revealed concerning them:

> Behold, how they devise a lie against God; and therein is iniquity sufficiently manifest ... They believe in fake gods and idols, and say of those who believe not, "These are more rightly guided in the Way than they who believe."
>
> Q. 4: 49-55

Thus puffed up, the Quraysh agreed to join forces with them and to eradicate what they considered the source of all their problems. The Jews then went to Ghatafan, informed them of the decision the Quraysh had made and the preparation they were making to fight the Muslims, spurred them to join forces with them, and promised them their own support. So, a large force of ten thousand by some accounts, twelve thousand by other accounts was assembled by the Quraysh and the Ghatafan, to attack Madinah from the south and from the north.

Meanwhile Huyayy went to Ka'b ibn Asad of the Banu Qurayza to persuade him to break his covenant with the Prophet and join the new alliance between the Quraysh and the Ghatafan. Ka'b refused to break his pact with Muhammad and help his enemies, saying, "I have always found him

(Muhammad) loyal and faithful." Huyayy kept on pushing and persuading until Ka'b relented and promised to kill Muhammad if the Quraysh and the Ghatafan were unable to do so, thus breaking his pact with the Apostle.

It is said that when the Apostle heard of these preparations, upon the advice of Salman, the Parsi (Persian) he ordered a ditch to be dug around the city. He himself undertook the task and the Muslims rallied behind him working with all the zeal and energy they could muster. Strange accounts have been recorded of miraculous events in the course of the digging of the trench. How in one instance when a large rock impeded their task, the Apostle called for some water, spat in it, said a prayer and poured the water on the rock whereupon the rock pulverized. And, how on another occasion, the Prophet took a handful of dates from a girl who was carrying it to her father and uncle, spread it on a sheet of cloth, invited all the workers to lunch, and how they all had their fill while the dates kept increasing so that in the end there was still plenty left, reminiscent of the feeding of about five thousand with five loaves of the barley bread and two fishes by his Holiness Jesus Christ.

The account of Salman, however, is very interesting as it foretells of future events in the course of Islamic history. "I was working with a Pick in the trench," narrates Salman, "When a rock gave me much trouble. The Apostle, passing by, saw me heaving hard, dropped down into the ditch, took the pick from me and gave a hard blow upon the rock. Lightning flashed beneath the pick. A second and a third blow followed, producing lightning similar to the first. I said, 'O Messenger of God! What is the meaning of this light that flashes under the pick every time you strike?' He said, 'Did you really see that, Salman? The first indicates my victory over the Yeman; the second Syria and the West; the third the East!' " Yeman was subdued by 'Alí in the tenth year of the Hijrah; Syria, the West and the East were conquered during the Caliphates of 'Umar, 'Uthman, the Ummayyads and the 'Abbasids.

The Muslim army consisted of 3000 strong. The armies of the south and the north approached and confronted the ditch. This was a novel strategy in desert warfare which the Arabs had not experienced before. The hostile forces remained inactive, each on its side of the trench, for twenty days to a month, the archers shooting arrows at times with little effect. However, the formidable force looked awesome and several of the faint-hearted Muslims took to their heels. The disaffection became so serious that the Apostle sent an emissary to the leaders of Ghatafan offering them a third of the dates of Madinah on conditon that they would return to their country in Hijaz. While the document for this agreement was being prepared the Prophet sought the advice of the two Sa'ds, leaders of Aus and Khazraj tribes to whom belonged the dates he was negotiating with the enemy. They asked him whether this was a command he had received from God or it was his own policy for the security of Madinah. The Apostle said, "By God it is something I want to do for you, seeing that the Arabs have surrounded us bent on our destruction." The leader of the Khazraj said, "O Prophet of God! When we were all polytheists, these people could enjoy eating our dates only as guests or by purchase. Now that we have been honoured by Islám, can we allow them to have our property and relish it with impunity? We will give them nothing but the sword until God decide between us." "Let them do their worst against us," said Muhammad, and tore the as yet unsigned document.

'Amr ibn 'Abdu Wudd, 'Ikrimah ibn Abu Jahl and a few other horsemen of the Quraysh found a narrow pass in the trench, beat their horses through and challenged the Muslims to combat. 'Alí responded and killed 'Amr. The rest fled. This was the only skirmish in the battle of the Ditch.

Soon God decided the issue between the adversaries. A

devastating wind blew one cold night, blowing away tents, pots, pans and articles of clothing. Horses were running amock and many camels died. The disconcerted Quray<u>sh</u> and Ghatafan withdrew in haste. At dawn they were seen retiring hurriedly back to their respective lands. Six Muslims and three polytheists lost their lives in the battle of the Ditch.

THE FATE OF BANU QURAYZA

During the days when the opposing enemies took positions each on its side of the Ditch and watched each other's activities, when the Muslims were beleaguered from above and below, and several fearful and irresolute believers showed signs of disaffection, the Apostle looked for a way to sow the seeds of distrust and discord among his adversaries. Nu'aym of the Ghatafan had just become a Muslim, a fact not yet known to his relatives and friends. He was chosen by the Prophet and commissioned to carry out this scheme. He went to the Banu Qurayza, showed them his usual kindliness and deference; then in the course of conversation casually hinted of the danger of relying too much on the support of the Quraysh and the Ghatafan. "This is your land and your property where your wives and children live," he told them. "If things go badly with the Quraysh and the Ghatafan, they will return to their respective land, leaving you here at the mercy of Muhammad and the Muslims. The least you can do is to demand that they turn over to you a number of their chiefs to stand surety in the event that the battle runs against them and they take to their heels leaving you in the lurch." They agreed that it was sound advice and they would act on it.

Nu'aym then went to the Quraysh, and under the guise of friendship and special consideration for their interests he told them he had come to warn them of a plot brewing in the Banu Qurayza camp against them and the Ghatafan. But they should keep it confidential. "Mark my words," he told them, "the Jews have regretted their action in opposing Muhammad and have sent an envoy to make a deal with him. Their message to him was: 'Would you like us to get hold of some chiefs of the two tribes Quraysh and Ghatafan and hand them over to you so that you can cut their heads off? Then we can join you in exterminating the rest of them.' Muhammad has sent word back accepting their offer; so if the Jews send to you to demand hostages, don't send them a single man." Nu'aym then warned Ghatafan in a similar manner.

The Quraysh and the Ghatafan then sent Ikrimah ibn Abu Jahl to the Banu Qurayza to tell them that their men were suffering in the cold winter nights in their temporary camps, that their horses and camels were dying and that it was imperative that the Jews make ready for an onrush against Muhammad and make an end of him. This message arrived on the night of the Sabbath. The Jews said they would not and could not violate the Sabbath of the Lord. "Moreover," they said, "we will not fight Muhammad along with you, until you give us hostages whom we hold as security until we make an end of Muhammad: for we fear that if the battle goes against you and you suffer heavily you will withdraw at once to your country and leave us while the man (meaning the Prophet) is in our country, and we cannot face him alone." When the tribes received the reply they said, "Now we know that what Nu'aym told us was the truth." So, they did not send them a single man and said, "If they want to fight let them come out and fight." When the Jews received this message, they said: "What Nu'aym told us was the truth." They sent word that they would not attack Muhammad unless they had hostages.

We know, of course, that God protected His Messenger and the Muslims by sending the wind which caused havoc in the camps of their adversaries. But the Apostle's scheme brought out the duplicity and treachery of the Banu Qurayza into the open. It was made clear to all that they broke their contract with Muhammad and had every intention of destroying him if the opportunity was favourable. It is said that Gabriel appeared to him and said, "God commands you,

Muhammad, to go to Banu Qurayza. I am about to go to them to shake their stronghold." The Muslims laid siege on them for twenty-five nights until they surrendered to the Apostle in sheer exhaustion and desperation.

Now Huyayy ibn Akhtab, the arch mischief-maker, was in their fort when Ka'b, the leader of the Banu Qurayza gave his tribesmen three choices. (1) Accept Islám, for it has become evident that Muhammad is the Prophet foretold in our scriptures. By doing so, we shall save ourselves, our women, our children and our property. "We will never abandon the laws of the Torah and never change it for another," they said. (2) Let us kill our women and children, unsheathe our swords and rush the Muslims. We shall either perish in which case we shall have no anxiety about our women and children; we shall defeat Muhammad in which case we can marry other women and have children. "What would be the good of life after we kill these poor creatures?" they said. (3) Tonight is the eve of the Sabbath. Muhammad and his companions may be relaxing, knowing we shall take no action on the Sabbath. Let us surprise them; perhaps, we shall take them unawares and kill them. "Are we to profane our Sabbath and do what is unlawful?" They had no other option but to submit to Muhammad's judgment. In their pre-Islamic days they had an alliance with the tribe of al-Aus and sought their help now. The Aus interceded in their behalf, and the Apostle agreed to arbitration. Sa'd, a leader of the Aus, was appointed umpire by them and the Prophet agreed to respect his decision in the matter. They told Sa'd, "Deal kindly with your friends, for the Apostle has accepted your judgment for that very purpose."

When Sa'd came to the assembled Madinans ('Emigrants', and 'Helpers'), they all got up as a sign of respect. Sa'd asked them, "Do you covenant by God that you accept the judgment I pronounce on them?" They said, "Yes." Then turning to the Apostle, but not mentioning him by name, he said, "And is it incumbent on the one who is here?" The Apostle said, "Yes." Sa'd then said, "I give judgment that the men should be killed, the property divided, and the women and children taken as captives."

Six hundred or Seven hundred men[93] were taken in batches and slain by the sword. When Huyayy was brought out, he said to the Apostle, "By God, I do not blame myself for opposing you, but he who forsakes God will be forsaken." Then he added, "God's command is right. A Book and a Decree, and massacre have been written against the sons of Israel!" Then he sat down and his head was struck off.

God revealed concerning this episode in Sura 33 'The Confederates', Vs. 7-27. He reminded the Jews of their covenants with the Prophets, saying, "And (We) received from them a firm covenant; that We may examine the speakers of truth concerning their veracity[94];" He then addressed the Muslims:

> O true believers! remember the favour of God towards you, when armies came against you, and We sent against them a wind, and hosts which ye saw not: and God beheld that which ye did ... when your sight became troubled, and your hearts came even to your throats... And the hypocrites and the diseased in heart said, 'God and His Apostle made us only false promises,' and a part of them said, 'O people of Yathrib! You cannot stand against them; so return to your houses.' And a part of them asked leave of the Apostle, saying, 'Verily, our houses are left defenceless.' And they were not defenceless, their intention was no other than to run away. ...Say: Flight shall not profit you ...

---

[93] In a Tablet addressed to an early believer Bahá'u'lláh, giving a summary of this episode, states, ".... in two days they slew seven hundred men..."

Iqtindarat, P.125.

[94] See deut. 18:18-22.

Who is he who will defend you against God, if He wills evil for you, or is pleased to show mercy towards you? ... And He has caused such of those who have received the Scriptures (the Jews), who had aided the Confederates (The Quray<u>sh</u> and the Ghatafan), to come down out of their fortresses, and He cast into their hearts terror and dismay: a part ye slew and a part ye made captives; and God has caused you to inherit their land, and their houses, and their wealth...

THE RAID ON BANU AL-MUSTALIQ

News came that the Banu al-Mustaliq were gathering a force to attack the Prophet. A Muslim force was equipped and met them at their watering place. The Banu al-Mustaliq were put to flight; some of their men were killed, their women and children were taken captive and were distributed among the Muslims. This was a short defensive measure of no great significance. However, the incidents that followed are matters of interest.

Two men fell into fighting over which had the right to drink first from a well. One called the 'Helpers' to his aid; the other called the 'Emigrants'. 'Abdullah ibn Ubayy, the arch-liar, found a favourable opportunity to drive a wedge between the original inhabitants of Madinah, the 'Helpers', and the Quraysh 'Emigrants'. He said "They (meaning the 'Emigrants') outnumber us in our own country. As the saying goes, 'Feed a dog and it will devour you'. By God, when we return to Madinah the stronger will drive out the weaker." Then upbraiding the 'Helpers', he added, "This is what you have done to yourselves. You have let them occupy your country, and you have divided your property among them. Had you but kept your property from them they would have gone elsewhere."

When this was reported to the Prophet, 'Umar was with him and advised him to have 'Abdullah killed. "No!" replied the Apostle, "People will say Muhammad kills his own people". He ordered the Muslims to move on the Madinah. 'Abdullah ibn Ubayy went to the Apostle and denied the report. The 'Helpers', too, said that possibly the reporter made a mistake. A more judicious friend who heard about 'the stronger driving out the weaker', told the Apostle. "But you will drive him out if you want to: he is the weak and you are the strong. Then he added, "Treat him kindly, for God brought you to us when people were stringing beads to make him a crown, and he thinks that you have deprived him of a kingdom."

God revealed concerning this matter:

They say: If we return to Madinah, the stronger will drive the weaker therefrom; and might belongs to God and His Messenger and the believers, but the hypocrites know (it) not. O true believers, let not your riches or your children divert you from the remembrance of God: for whosoever doth this, they will surely be losers.

Q. 63: 8, 9

If two parties of the believers contend with one another, do ye compose the matter between them... and make peace between them with equity: and act with justice; for God loveth those who act justly. Verily the true believers are brethren: wherefore reconcile your brethren.

Q. 49: 9, 10

The Apostle showed extreme forbearance and dealt kindly with 'Abdullah ibn Uhayy and the parties were reconciled.

During the battle with Banu al-Mustaliq, a Muslim killed another Muslim called Hisham ibn Subaba by mistake. Miqyas, Hisham's brother, came from Makkah, professed to be a Muslim and asked payment of blood-money for his brother's murder. The Prophet ordered him paid, and showed him hospitality for a few days. Miqyas then killed the slayer of his brother and took off to Makkah. But he did not escape God's punishment, for in AH 8, when Makkah was occupied, his name was on the list of those who were to be beheaded. He was killed by Numayla, one of his own tribe.

Another incident of interest related to Juwayriya daughter of al-Harith, chief of Banu al-Mustaliq. According to 'A'isha, "she was a most beautiful woman. She captivated every man who saw her." When the captives were distributed among the men, she fell to the lot of Thabit, and she gave him a deed for her redemption. One day she appeared at the Prophet's door. "You can see the state to which I have been brought," she told the Apostle, "I have fallen to the lot of Thabit or his cousin and have given him a deed for my ransom and have come to ask your help in the matter." The Prophet offered her something she could not refuse. "I will discharge your debt and marry you", he told her, and she immediately accepted his proposal.

The marriage made Banu Mustaliq the Prophet's kith and kin. According to their standards and their perception of cultural values, this introduced a new outlook and behaviour in their social relationship. The Muslims freed the captives. Nearly a hundred families, thus released, were able to go back to their homes. All of them became Muslims. The Apostle then sent al-Walid ibn 'Uqba to teach them, to recite the Qur'án to them, and to collect the poor tax according to the precepts of Islám. The new converts to Islám rode out to meet their teacher as a sign of respect. Al-Walid, however, thought they intended to kill him, and fled to Madinah. He reported to the Prophet that the people were bent on killing him and refused to pay poor tax. A delegation arrived and explained matters to the Prophet: "We heard about your messenger", they explained, "We went out to meet him to show him respect and to pay the poor tax that was due, and he went back as fast as he could. Now we hear that he has alleged that we went out to kill him. God is our witness we did not go out with such intent." God revealed concerning this incident:

O true believers! if a wicked man come unto you with a tale, inquire strictly (into the truth thereof); lest ye hurt people through ignorance, and afterwards repent of what ye have done.

Q. 49: 6

Another incident which took place in the aftermath of the foray against the Banu Mustaliq concerned 'A'isha, the Prophet's wife, and will be the subject of our next story.

DEFAMATION OF CHARACTER LEADS TO SERIOUS CONSEQUENCES

The choice of which wife would accompany the Apostle on his expedition was usually made by casting lots among them. On the expedition against the Banu Mastaliq, the lot fell on 'A'isha. The Apostle's wife sat in a hawdah[95] which was lifted, put on the camel's back and strapped to it. To avoid the heat of the day, the force travelled by night. At the last station before Madinah, 'A'isha left her hawdah and moved off on a private occasion. She was wearing a necklace of onyxes of Zafar. When she returned to her camel she noticed the necklace was not around her neck. She went in search of it, found it and returned only to find that the men had gone and not a soul was there. The men in charge of her camel, thinking that she was sitting in her hawdah, had lifted it to the camel's back, strapped it, and moved off with the troops. She bundled herself up in her wrapper and lay by the roadside, confident they would come for her when they realized she was missing.

A young rider, called Safwan, had also fallen behind the main body. He spotted her lying on the desert sand. He recognized the Apostle's wife, put her on his camel and, leading the camel, proceeded as fast as he could. He caught up with the men at noon the next day, when they were resting. 'Abdullah ibn Ubayy, always on the lookout to find an opportunity to hurt the Apostle, spread the report, accusing 'A'isha of false doing. A handful of men fanned the flame, whispered all manner of unfounded accusations disturbing the army.

---

[95] A litter (with a covering and curtains) in which a person sits or relaxes while being carried on the back of an animal.

'A'isha herself had no notion of what was going on. She became ill immediately after her return from the expedition, was taken to her parent's house and lay in bed for nearly twenty days. All she noticed was that the Apostle did not show his usual affection towards her, which was most disconcerting, particularly at a time when she needed it most. She learned about the whole affair several days after her recovery when a friend told her about it. She wept a great deal and told her mother, "God forgive you! Men have spoken ill of me, and you have known of it and have not told me a thing about it." "My little daughter," answered her mother, "don't let the matter weigh on you. Seldom is there a beautiful woman married to a man who loves her but her rival wives gossip about her and men do the same."

The Messenger of God was much perturbed by a scandal implicating his own wife. Meanwhile the two rival tribes in Madinah, the Aus and the K̲h̲azraj each blamed the other for circulating false accusations, demanding punishment of death for the culprits. The rift grew wider as feeling ran higher and there was danger that fighting would flare up between them. The story, as related by 'A'isha, is that the Apostle consulted with Usamah and 'Alí; the former praised 'A'isha and said the accusations were false and lies, while the latter said, "Women are plentiful, and you can easily change one for another," and suggested that the Apostle seek the truth by questioning 'A'isha's slave girl[96]. The Apostle then talked directly with His wife. " A'isha," He said to her, "you know what people say about you. Fear God and if you have done wrong as men say then repent towards God, for He accepts repentence from His slaves." But confident of her innocence she said, "Never will I repent towards God of what you

---

[96] Historians consider this episode to be the source of 'A'isha's hatred of 'Alí. She never forgave him and years later joined forces with Talhah and al-Zubayr against him at al-Basrah. In the battle, called 'the battle of the camel', after 'A'isha's camel, both men lost their lives, 'A'isha was captured, treated generously and returned to Madinah.

mention. By Alláh, I know that if I were to confess what men say of me, God knowing that I am innocent of it, I should admit what did not happen; and if I denied what they said you would not believe me." Then she recited from the Qur'án what Jacob had said when Joseph's brothers "produced his inner garment stained with false blood." "Patience is most becoming, and God's assistance is to be implored."[97]

And in truth God's Revelation came to His Apostle. As to the party among you who have published the falsehood, think it not to be an evil unto you. To every man of them shall it be done according to the offence; and he among them who hath undertaken to aggravate the same, shall suffer a grievous punishment[98]. Did not the faithful men, and the faithful women, when ye heard this, think well of their own people, and say: This is a manifest falsehood? Have they produced four witnesses thereof? Wherefore since they have not produced the witnesses, they are surely liars in the sight of God... When ye published that with your tongues, and spoke that with your mouths, of which ye had no knowledge; and esteemed it to be a light matter, but with God it was a grave one. When ye heard it, did ye say, "It befits us not to talk of this matter: God forbid! this is a grievous calumny?"

Q. 24: 11-16

The people who spread the scandal were 'Abdullah ibn Ubayy, Mistah, Hassan and Hamna, the sister of Zaynab, the Prophet's wife. The last three were flogged eighty stripes each. 'Abdullah ibn Ubayy was spared, although he was the original instigator and the ringleader, because the Apostle was apparently averse to disgracing him publicly, he being a chief of his people. Judgment, in his case, was left to God. When in A.H. 9, he bacame ill and was dying, his son asked

---

[97] Sur. 12:18
[98] 'Abdullah ibn Ubayy

the Apostle to beg forgiveness for him from God. The Apostle complied. God revealed:

> Ask forgiveness for them, or do not ask forgiveness for them (it will be equal). If thou ask forgiveness for them seventy times, God will by no means forgive them. This for that they believe not in God and His Messenger; and God guides not the ungodly people.
>
> Q. 9: 80

Abu Bakr used to give an allowance to Mistah who was a relative and needy. He swore he would stop the allowance as he had brought so much sorrow and pain to them. God revealed concerning this:

> Let not the possessors of grace and abundance among you swear that they will not give unto kindred, and the poor, and those who have fled their country for the sake of God's true religion; but let them forgive, and act with benevolence. Do ye not desire that God should pardon you?
>
> Q. 24: 22

Abu Bakr resumed his support.

And finally, a short anecdote and a lesson on gossip and backbiting. Abu Ayyub's wife said to him, "Have you heard what people are saying about 'A'isha?" "Certainly, but it is a lie," he said, "would you do such a thing?" he asked. "No, by Alláh, I would not," she answered with confidence. "Well, 'A'isha is a better woman than you."

THE CONVERSION OF 'AMR IBN AL-'AS AND KHALID IBN AL-WALID

Khalid ibn al-Walid reported by some Arab historians as 'the sword of Alláh', and 'Amr ibn al-'AS, were two stalwart men of Quraysh whose spectacular valour in the wars that took place during the Caliphate of Abu Bakr and 'Umar gained vast territories for Islám, and who in recent times earned the tribute of a prominent historian who wrote: "The military campaigns of Khalid ibn al-Walid and 'Amr ibn al-'AS which ensued in al-Iraq, Persia, Syria and Egypt are among the most brilliantly executed in the history of warfare and bear favourable comparison with those of Napoleon, Hannibal or Alexander."[99]

But these two champions of the Faith and heroes of Muslim expansion were the enemies of the Messenger of God before accepting Islám. Khalid was the commander of the Cavalry at the battle of Uhud, which adroitly turned the defeat of the Quraysh into a resounding victory for them. 'Amr was the man that the Quraysh had sent to the Negus of Abyssinia to persuade to expel the Muslims from his territory. Both had participated in the battle of the Ditch against the Muslims.

Now, immediately after the battle of the Ditch, 'Amr gathered a number of his friends and associates in Makkah and told them that in his opinion the affair of Muhammad would be long-drawn. He suggested that they should go to Abyssinia with gifts and stay in that country. If Muhammad gained victory, they would rather be living in the protection of the Negus than under Muhammad's rule. If the Quraysh won, they could return to their own land and people. Thus he was

---

[99] History of the Arabs', by Philip K. Hitti, Tenth Edition, p. 142.

able to persuade a part of the Quray<u>sh</u> to seek hospitality in Abyssinia.

When 'Amr arrived at the Negus's court to seek an audience and offer his presents, he saw 'Amr ibn Umayya, an envoy of the Prophet, leave the Court. He thought if he could lay hold of him and kill him, he would be doing a great service to the Quray<u>sh</u> which might fare well with him at a later date. So, after doing the customary obeissance to the Negus and renewing his acquaintance with him, he said, "O King! I have just seen a man leave your presence. He is the messenger of an enemy of ours, so let me have him that I may kill him, for he has killed some of our chiefs and best men." The Negus was so enraged that he struck him a blow on his nose, and said angrily, "Would you ask me to give you the messenger of a man to whom the great Namus[100] comes as it used to come to Moses, so that you might kill him! Woe to you, 'Amr, obey me and follow him, for by God, he is right and will triumph over his adversaries as Moses triumphed over Pharaoh and his armies." These words overwhelmed him. He suddenly realized the error of his judgment, and begged the Negus to accept his allegiance to the Apostle. He then stretched out his hand and the Negus accepted his allegiance to Muhammad and to Islám.

Much later, on his way to Madinah to pay homage to the Apostle of God, he met Khalid coming from Makkah. This must have been in the eighth year of the Hijra, a little while before the occupation of Makkah. "Where are you going, Abu Sulayman?" he asked Khalid, to which the latter replied, "The way has become clear. The man is certainly a prophet, and by God I'm going to be a Muslim. How much longer should I delay?" They both sought the same goal. They gave their

---

[100] A word that has probably come from the Greek nomos, meaning law. Some ascribe it to the Torah (the Mosaic laws); some to Gabriel who descended from God with Revelations. In Persian and Arabic, it conveys other meanings too.

allegiance to the Prophet and asked forgiveness for their past misdeeds. The Prophet said, "Islám does away with all that preceded it, as does the Hijra."

THE PACT OF AL HUDAYBIYYAH, A DECLARATION OF PEACE

In the month of Dhu'l-Qa'dah, A.H. 6, the Apostle decided to go on Pilgrimage to the Ka'bah in Makkah. Seven hundred, some say 1400, others say as many as 4400 of the 'Emigrants' and the 'Helpers' and other Arabs accompanied him on his pilgrimage. Seventy camels were taken to be sacrificed, one for each ten pilgrims. They donned the pilgrim garbs, as a clear indication that their intention was a peaceful visit to the Ka'bah. At 'Usfan, report came that the Quraysh were suspicious of their true intentions, resented their entry into Makkan territory without their consent and were out in great numbers with their women and children on the war path, having sent out their cavalry under Khalid ibn al-Walid in their advance.

The Apostle became sad, and said, "What are the Quraysh thinking of? Is killing me their only desire? They know that if God gives me victory, they will enter Islám in troops, and I will not cease to fight for the mission with which God has entrusted me until He makes it victorious or I perish." To avoid confrontation with the Quraysh, he decided to take a different way. A guide took them through rugged country and rocky mountain passes until they reached easier ground. They glorified God and asked His forgiveness. They advanced towards Makkah and encamped at al-Hudaybiyah, some seven miles north of the city. At the Apostle's command a hole was dug and they struck water for their use and for their camels. The Quraysh sent several emissaries, one following the other, to inquire after Muhammad's real intention. To each the same message was given that the purpose was a peaceful pilgrimage to the Ka'bah. But the Quraysh refused to believe the reports brought by their own emissaries. One of them

'Urwah who had been asked to see for signs of disaffection among the companions could not believe his eyes when he saw the homage and servility shown the Apostle by them, how they ran to get the water he had used in his ablutions, how they would pick up a hair that fell off his head and with what veneration they preserved it. He told the Quraysh, "I have been to Chosroes in his kingdom, and Caesar in his kingdom and the Negus in his kingdom, but never have I seen a king among a people like Muhammad among his companions. I have seen a people who will never abandon him for any reason, so form your own opinion."

Finally the Quraysh sent Suhayl ibn 'Amr with a mandate to conclude a pact to make peace on condition that the pilgrims would return to Madinah and come the following year. This was done in order that the Quraysh may save face so that the tribes may not say the Quraysh were forced to admit them. When the Apostle agreed to make peace, many of the companions considered this a let down, and felt offended and humiliated. 'Umar went to Abu Bakr, saying, "Is He not God's Apostle, and are we not Muslims, and are they not polytheists? Why should we agree to what is demeaning to our religion? "Stick to what he says," replied Abu Bakr, "for I testify that he is God's Apostle." 'Umar then said that he, too, testified to that. And when he put the question to the Apostle, he replied, "I am God's slave and His Apostle. I will not go against His commandment, and He will not make me a loser." 'Umar was put to shame for thinking that his opinion was better than God's, and tried to make amends the rest of his life by praying and fasting and paying alms and freeing slaves.

At the Apostle's behest, a document was written by 'Ali, which stipulated a ten year truce, right of annual pilgrimage for the Muslims, freedom of both parties to enter into bonds and agreements with third parties. The Apostle also agreed to return to Makkah anyone coming to him without his guardian's permission, without a similar reciprocal condition for the Quraysh.

On the face of it, it seemed to be a humiliating arrangement for the Muslims. However God revealed:

Verily, We have granted thee a manifest victory: that God may forgive thee thy preceding and thy subsequent sin, and may complete His favour on thee, and direct thee in the right way; and that God may assist thee with a glorious assistance... Verily We have sent thee to be a witness and a bearer of good tidings, and a denouncer of threats; that ye may believe in God and His Apostle, and may assist him and revere him, and praise him morning and evening. Verily, they who swear fealty unto thee, swear fealty unto God...

Q. 48: 1-3; 8-10

Commenting on the consequence of this pact, Ibn Ishaq says: "No previous victory in Islám was greater than this. There was nothing but battle when men met; but when there was an armistice and war was abolished and men met in safety and consulted together none talked about Islám intelligently without entering it. In those two years (A.H. 6-A.H. 8 the Conquest of Makkah) double as many or more than double as many entered Islám as ever before."

LETTERS TO THE KINGS

During the year A.H. 6, the Apostle sent a number of letters to the Kings and Rulers calling them to God and to Islám.

To Heraclius, the Byzantine Emperor, a letter was sent with Dihyah ibn Khalifa al-Kalbi. The text of the letter as handed down to us is this:

In the name of God, the Compassionate, the Merciful! Muhammad who is the servant of God, and His Apostle, to Harqal, the Qaisar of Rome[101]. Peace be on whoever has gone on the straight path. Verily I call you to Islám. Embrace Islám and God will reward you twofold. If you turn away from the offer of Islám, then on you be the sins of your people[102]. O people of the Book (referring to Christians) come towards the creed which is fit both for us and for you. It is this: to worship none but God, and not to associate anything with God, and not to call others God. Therefore, O ye people of the Book, if you refuse, beware! We are Muslims, and our religion is Islám.

Muhammad, the Apostle of God

It is said that Heraclius was greatly touched by the letter, investigated the claim of Muhammad and was convinced that he was God's Messenger, but his generals and the people refused to recognize him as a Messenger since they looked condescendingly at the Arabs and called them disparagingly people of sheep and camels, regarding them far inferior to themselves in civilization and refinement.

---

[101] Harqal is Arabic for Heraclius; Qaisar is Arabic for Ceasar; Rome was constantinople, the seat of the Byzantine Emperors.

[102] This means that due to his rejection, his people will also reject the Faith, and he shall bear the responsibility of their sin.

'Abdullah ibn Hudhafa was the Apostle's emissary to the Chosroes, the Shahanshah of the Persians. He was very discourteous to the emissary and irreverent to the Apostle since he tore up his letter after reading it. It is said that when the Apostle was apprised of this, he said, "His kingdom will be torn in pieces."

The Apostle sent 'Amr ibn Umayya al Damri to the Negus with this letter.

In the Name of God, the Compassionate, the Merciful. From Muhammad the Apostle of God to the Negus, King of Abyssinia, Peace. I praise Alláh, the King, the Holy, the Giver of Peace, the Faithful, the Guardian[103], and I bear witness that Jesus son of Mary is the spirit of God and His Word which He cast to Mary the virgin, the good, the pure, so that she conceived Jesus. God created him from His spirit and His breathing as He created Adam by His hand and His breathing. I call you to God the Unique without partner and to His obedience, and to follow me and to believe in that which came to me, for I am the Apostle of God... I have accomplished (my work) and my admonitions, so receive my advice. Peace upon all those that follow true guidance.

The Negus replied: "... From the Negus, Peace upon you, O Prophet of Alláh, and mercy and blessing from Alláh beside Whom there is no God, Who has guided me to Islám. I have received your letter in which you mention the matter of Jesus and by the Lord of heaven and earth he is not one scrap more than what you say... I testify that you are God's Apostle, true and confirming (those before you). I have given my fealty to you and to your nephew[104] and I have surrendered myself

---

[103] Extract from Sura 59: 23.

[104] The younger brother of 'Alí and a cousin of the Apostle who emigrated to Abyssinia and taught the teachings of Islám to the Negus.

through him to the Lord of the worlds..."

The Messenger of God sent letters to al-Mundhir, lord of Damascus, to Muqauqis, ruler of Alexandria, to al-Mundhir ibn Sawa, ruler of al-Bahrayn, and to the rulers of 'Uman, inviting each one of them to worship none but God, to recognize Him as His Messenger and to follow and obey him in the precepts of Islám as ordained by God.

THE EXPEDITION TO KHAYBAR, A.H. 7

About six days march to the north-east of Madinah lay a prosperous town inhabited by the Jews, called Khaybar. In his attempt to unify all the tribes in the Peninsula, to put an end to feuds and ties of protection, and to bring the whole of Arabia into the brotherhood of Islám, the Apostle now undertook an expedition against this well-fortified city. He equipped a force of about 1600 Muslims and marched out towards Khaybar. The Ghatafan, who inhabited the territory midway from Madinah to Khaybar, decided to help the Jews of Khaybar and a body of their men actually travelled north, but decided to return after a day's march fearing a Muslim attack on their tribe. The road was thus open for the Muslim army.

When the Apostle looked down on Khaybar, he recited this prayer:

"O God, Lord of the heavens and what they O'ershadow
And Lord of the Lands and what they make to grow
And Lord of the devils and what into error they throw
And Lord of the winds and what they winnow.
We ask Thee for the good of this town and the good of its people and the good of what is in it, and we take refuge in Thee from its evil and the evil of its people and the evil that is in it."

Then he commanded his companions, "Forward in the name of Alláh!"

Now several Jewish tribes lived each in its own fort in Khaybar. The Apostle conquered these one by one, seized their property and took their women and children captives.

The first to fall was the fort of Na'im. He took Safiya, daughter of his old enemy, Huyayy, for himself and married her. Some of the forts put up a good resistance and this made stringent demands upon the Muslims. Scarcity of food was the main difficulty, a condition that worsened as the resistance prolonged. They turned to the flesh of donkeys to satisfy their hunger. The Apostle prohibited this. A Muslim recounting his own experience, said later: "The Apostle's prohibition of the flesh of domestic donkeys reached us as the pots were boiling with it, so we turned them upside down." A few Muslims complained to the Apostle about the food shortage. He prayed to God for succour: "O God, You know their condition and that they have no strength, and that I have nothing to give them, so conquer for them the wealthiest of the enemy's forts with the richest food." The fort of al-Sa'b which contained the richest supply of food fell into their hands the following day.

The forts of al-Watih and al-Sulalim were the last two to be subdued. Marhab, a renowned Jewish warrior, and his brother Yasir came out and challenged the Muslims to single combat. Muhammad ibn Maslama responded to the challenge and proved a worthy match for Marhab. An old tree intervened between them. They hid behind it and circled around it striking blows at each other. When all the branches were cut off, the two warriors faced each other and exchanged blows. The end came when Muhammad gave the fatal blow which wounded and killed Marhab. Then al-Zubayr fought Yasir and killed him.

As usual in these expeditions 'Alí was the champion warrior of the Muslim forces and the bearer of the flag in the conquest of most of the forts. Abu Rafi', a freed slave of the Apostle recounted this personal observation: "We went with 'Alí when the Apostle sent him with His flag and when he got near the fort the garrison came out and he fought them. A Jew struck him so that his shield fell from his hand, so 'Alí laid hold of a door by the fort and used it as a shield. He kept it in his hand as he fought until God gave victory, throwing it away when all was over. I can see myself with seven others trying to turn that door over, but we could not." Of course, the anecdote is not free from the usual oriental exaggeration, but it goes to show 'Alí's valour as a fighter and the esteem in which he was held as a warrior.

With the surrender of the people of Khaybar, all their property fell prey to the Muslims, but the Jews asked the Apostle to employ them on the property with half share in the produce, and arrangement which was agreeable to the Apostle. The people of Fadak surrendered voluntarily without a fight. Their property came into the Apostle's personal possession and he made a similar arrangement with them regarding their employment. The spoils of some of the fortresses fell to the Muslims. Others were divided into sections benefitting a large number of the poor, orphans, wayfarers, the Apostle's wives, kindreds, men who had been in al-Hudaybiyah, but not at Khaybar, etc., etc.

During the days in Khaybar, the Apostle ordained four prohibitions:

1. Carnal intercourse with pregnant women taken captive.

2. Eating the flesh of domestic donkeys.

3. Eating any carnivorous animal.

4. Selling booty before it had been duly allotted.

THE EXPEDITION TO SYRIA A.H. 8

The last event of A.H. 7 was the Apostle's pilgrimage to Makkah, in fulfilment of the agreement reached the previous year at Hudaybiyah. He had intended to observe the complete rites of a pilgrimage, the Hajj, but the Quraysh expelled him from Makkah upon the completion of the third day. They were very unkind and discourteous to him. Even after he kindly invited them to his wedding feast with Maymuna d. al-Harith, they curtly replied, "We don't need your food, so get out!" Abu Rafi', his servant, brought Maymuna to Sarif where the marriage was consummated.

In the fifth month of the year A.H. 8, an army of 3000 men marched out towards Syria on an expedition known as Mu'ta, after the name of a village in Balqa' where they met Heraclius's force of 100,000 men.

Before engaging in battle against such a formidable force, they consulted for two nights. Some recommended writing to the Apostle asking him to send reinforcements or give directions. 'Abdullah ibn Rawaha said, "Men, what you dislike is that which you have come out in search of, namely, martyrdom. We are not fighting the enemy with numbers, or strength or multitude, but we are fighting them with this religion with which God has honoured us. So come on! Both prospects are fine: victory or martyrdom." Thus encouraged, the men decided to push forward, whatever the consequence.

The expedition proved a total disaster for the Muslims. They lost several of their best men — Zayd, the Prophet's adopted son, Ja'far ibn Abu Talib, 'Ali's younger brother, and 'Abdullah ibn Rawaha, an early believer and a trusted companion and confidant of the Prophet. These three were successively in command of the army and its standard bearers. As each fell, the next took over. They fought valiantly, but they were outnumbered over thirty to one and defeat was inevitable. When the third fell, the Muslims rallied to Khalid ibn al-Walid who prudently avoided engagement and retired taking the men away without much loss. The Apostle and his companions met the returning men as they approached Madinah. Some chided the men for turning tail and called them runaways, others threw dirt at them to show their indignation. The Apostle said, "They are not runaways, but come agains if God will." There was great lamentation in Madinah, and the Muslims mourned the death of the fallen of Mu'ta, particularly of their three heroes. A total of eight men of various clans, both of the 'Emigrants' and of the 'Helpers' died as martyrs at Mu'ta.

The Apostle was grieved over the companions that died in Mu'ta, particularly over Ja'far, his own cousin. It is said that he hugged Ja'far's sons and smelt them while his eyes filled with tears. He said to his family, "Do not neglect Ja'far's family. Send them food and console them while they are occupied with the disaster that has happened to their head.

THE CONQUEST OF MAKKAH A.H. 8

The truce concluded between the Apostle and the Makkan Quraysh stipulated that the contracting parties could give protection to the tribes that desired such a treaty relationship. A clan of Banu Bakr allied themselves with the Quraysh and the Khuza'a with the Apostle. The Banu Bakr then attacked the Khuza'a at night and killed one of them. Fighting continued and the Khuza'a were driven into the sacred area. Even then the Banu al-Dil did not desist. They were aided by the Quraysh with weapons and men. The Khuza'a then appealed to the Messenger to redress the wrong done to them.

The Quraysh sent Abu Sufyan to the Apostle to gain time as they were afraid of the consequence of what they had done. It is said that he went to his daughter Umm Habibah's house. Now Umm Habibah was one of the Apostle's wives. When he was about to sit on the floor, Umm Habibah folded up the carpet to prevent him from sitting on it. "My dear daughter," he said, "I hardly know if you think that the carpet is too good for me or that I am too good for the carpet!" She replied, " It is the Apostle's carpet and you are an unclean polytheist! I do not want you to sit on the Apostle's carpet." Surprised Abu Sufyan chided his daughter for her impertinence. Then he went to see the Apostle, but he would not speak to him. He then tried Abu Bakr who also refused to see him. 'Umar had harsh words for him. 'Alí and Fatimah were not unkind to him, but could not offer any useful advice as they deferred all matters to the Apostle's decision. Abu Sufyan returned to Makkah a disappointed man.

The Apostle found it necessary to take a positive and firm stance against the Quraysh for their breach of the covenant. He ordered mobilization and enjoined absolute secrecy. "O God," he said, "take eyes and ears from Quraysh so that we may take them by surprise in their land." The men went on with preparation for this expedition. A Muslim who had a son and other kin in Makkah and feared for their lives bribed a slave woman to carry a letter of warning to Quray<u>sh</u>. She was apprehended not long after she had set out. The man explained his reasons and appealed for forgiveness and mercy. He had fought at Badr and was forgiven. God revealed:

O true believers, take not My enemy and your enemy for friends, showing kindness toward them; since they believe not in the truth which hath come unto you, having expelled the Apostle and yourselves (from Makkah your native city) because ye believe in God, your Lord. If you go forth to fight in defence of My religion, and out of a desire to please Me, and privately show friendship unto them; verily I will know that which ye conceal, and that which ye discover; and whoever of you doth this, hath already erred from the straight path. If they get the better of you, they will be enemies unto you, and they will stretch forth their hands and their tongues against you with evil; and they earnestly desire that ye should become unbelievers. Neither your kindred nor your children will avail you at all on the Day of Resurrection, which will separate you from one another: and God seeth that which ye do. Ye have an excellent pattern in Abraham, and those who were with him, when they said unto their people, "Verily we are clear of you, and of that which ye worship, besides God: we have renounced you; and enmity and hatred is begun between us and you forever, until ye believe in God alone." Except Abraham's saying unto his father, "Verily I will beg pardon for thee; but I cannot obtain aught of God in thy behalf." O Lord, in Thee do we trust, and unto Thee are we turned; and to Thee is the eventual coming.

Q. 60: 1-4

The army marched out. The 'Emigrants' and the 'Helpers' formed the main body; not one of them stayed behind. Men from other tribes joined in and the number swelled to about 10,000 Muslims. Naturally a force of this size travelling over 12 days is full of incidents and numerous interesting anecdotes could be recounted. But we cannot dwell on them lest the chapter be prolonged beyond the scope of our chronicle. Al-'Abbas, the Apostle's uncle, brought Abu Sufyan to him in one of the stations on the road to Makkah, and interceded in his behalf. The Prophet said to him when he was brought to his presence, "Isn't it time that you should recognize that there is no God but Alláh?" He answered: "You are dearer to me than father and mother. How great is your clemency, honour and kindness! By God, I thought that had there been another god with God he would have continued to help me." Then the Apostle said to him, "Woe to you, Abu Sufyan, isn't it time that you recognize that I am God's Apostle?" And he answered: "As to that I still have some doubt." Al-'Abbas told him, "Submit and testify that there is no god but Alláh and that Muhammad is the Apostle of God before you lose your head," and so he did. He then returned to his people in Makkah fully impressed by Muhammad's following and their loyalty and complete obedience to his every command. He told them that resistance was no longer possible. It would only lead to unnecessary and fruitless bloodshed. He counselled them to take refuge in their homes and in the mosque. The Quraysh even then were full of hatred towards Muhammad, and cursed and abused Abu Sufyan. 'Utba, seizing his moustaches, cried, "Kill this fat greasy bladder of lard; this rotten protector of the people!" For eighteen years they had fought Muhammad by every weapon in their arsenal. And now they saw the enemy that slipped from their grip when they plotted to kill him eight years earlier return commanding thousands of loyal supporters against whom they had no option but to bow and to surrender. The Apostle of God entered Makkah in a three-pronged formation, the right wing and the main body faced no resistance, but the left wing under Khalid ibn al-Walid encountered slight opposition at al-Khandama leading to a skirmish in which 12 or 13 polytheists and 2 Muslims lost their lives. This opposition was raised by Safwan ibn Umayya, 'Ikrima ibn Abu Jahl, and Suhayl ibn 'Amr. Muhammad had instructed his army commanders to exercise patience and to make every effort to reduce bloodshed, not to attack, but to defend. Only a small number of hypocrites and gross defectors and a few with a history of crimes of rapacity, plunder and murder were ordered killed.

It is said that the Aposlte summoned the custodian of the Ka'ba and ordered its door to be opened. When he entered he found there a dove made of wood. He crushed it in his hand and threw it away. He then had the 360 idols in the Ka'ba destroyed, reciting the verse in the Qur'án, "The truth has come and falsehood has passed away; verily falsehood is sure to pass away." (Q.17:81) The idols around the Ka'bah were also collected and burnt. All, but the pictures of Jesus and Mary, were erased. He then stood at the door of the Ka'bah and said, "There is no God but Allah alone; He has no associate. He has made good His promise and helped His servant. He has put to flight the confederates alone. Every claim of privilege[105] or blood or property are abolished by me except the custody of the Temple and the watering of the pilgrims. The unintentionally slain in a quasi-intentional way by club or whip[106], for him the bloodwit is most severe: a hundred camels, 40 of them to be pregnant. O Quraysh, God has taken from you the haughtiness of paganism and its veneration of ancestors. Man springs from Adam and Adam sprang from dust." Then he recited this verse: 'O men, We created you from male and female and made you into peoples and tribes, that you may know one another: of a truth the most noble of you, in God's sight is the most pious of you...'[107] He then asked

---

[105] Especially inherited authority.

[106] i.e. manslaughter..

them what they thought he would do with them. They said, "Good. You are a noble brother, son of a noble brother," He said, "Go your way for you are the freed ones!"

A ceremony followed during which the Makkans paid homage to the Apostle of God, while he sat on al-Safa, promising to hear and obey God and His Apostle to the best of their ability. To the women he enjoined obedience to God and His Apostle, not to associate anything with God, not to steal, not to commit adultery, not to kill their children, and not to invent slanderous tales. He then asked 'Umar to accept their troth and asked God's forgiveness for them.

Abu Bakr brought his father, now much advanced in age and almost blind, to the Apostle to accept Islám and pay homage to the Apostle. Muhammad was very gracious to him and reproached Abu Bakr, saying, "Why did you not leave the old man in his house so that I could come to him there?"

Muhammad forgave Hind for what she had done to Hamza at Uhud, when she approached the Apostle to pay homage and accept Islám. Safwan and 'Ikrima were also forgiven their past errors through the intercession of their wives who had accepted Islám. They, too, accepted Islám, and the Apostle confirmed their marriages.

Thus ended peacefully a prolonged conflict between the Apostle and the Makkan Quraysh paving the way for the establishment of the commonwealth of Islám in the Arabian Peninsula.

After the occupation of Makkah in the month of Ramadan of A.H. 8, the Prophet stayed there about a fortnight and, being informed that Hawazin and Thaqif had assembled a large force to attack Quraysh and were encamped at Hunayn, a valley about six kilometres east of Makkah, he marched out against them.

---

[107] Q. 49:13

THE BATTLE OF HUNAYN, A.H. 8

Before embarking on the above incident two events ought to be mentioned briefly.

One relates to the expedition that the Apostle ordered Khalid ibn al-Walid to undertake to the Banu Jadhima country to invite them to God. The purpose was purely missionary, and the Apostle had made it clear that there would be no fighting. Khalid, however, went beyond the Apostle's clear instructions, and a peaceful mission turned into vengeful killing of a number of the tribe. When the chilling report reached the Apostle, he was flabbergasted, raised his hands to heaven and said, "O God, I am innocent before Thee of what Khalid has done." He sent 'Alí to redress the wrong and to teach the tribe to abandon the practices of the pagan era. 'Alí left with money, paid the necessary bloodwit and made a generous compensation for the wrong done.

The second relates to the destruction of al-'Uzza in Nakhla, a temple venerated by some of the adjoining tribes. It is said that when the custodian of the temple heard of the approach of the Muslims, he hung his sword on her and fled to the mountains, saying:

O 'Uzza, make an annihilating attack on Khalid,
Throw aside your your veil and gird up your train,
O 'Uzza, if you do not kill this man Khalid,
Then bear a swift punishment or become a Muslim.

Khalid destroyed the temple and returned to Makkah.

All the clans of Hawazin except Ka'b and Kilab, assembled under Malik ibn Auf their chief. They were joined by the two clans of Thaqif — the Ahlaf led by Qarib, and the Banu Malik led by two brothers Dhu'l-Khimar and Ahmar. Malik ibn Auf was recognized as the commander of the combined tribes. Now, when they heard that the Apostle had left Madinah at the head of a mighty army, they thought his intention was to attack them, and so they started preparations to fight. But then they heard of the conquest of Makkah, and Malik decided to attack the Prophet, and to make sure that his men, some 4000 strong, would stand their ground against the enemy, he ordered their wives, children and cattle march behind them. They then marched towards Makkah and encamped in the valley of Hunayn, a short distance from that city. Malik ordered his men to break their scabbards, as soon as they saw the enemy, and attack them as one man.

The Apostle gathered an army of 12,000 men — 2000 of the Makkan Quray<u>sh</u> and 10,000 of the companions and believers that had come from Madinah for the conquest of Makkah. He borrowed weapons and armour from Safwan, a polytheist at the time, who agreed to provide them with his own transport. They rejoiced in their great numbers and thought they would be invincible.

The battle went against the Muslims, at first. The enemy had taken positions behind rocks and mountain crags and narrow openings and as they unexpectedly attacked en-masse, the heathen Quray<u>sh</u> — just converted to Islám with little confidence in the Apostle — were terrified, turned tail and fled causing confusion and constrernation, the camels bumping into each other. Many still bore their grudge against the Apostle. Abu Sufyan ibn Harb said disparagingly, "Their flight will not stop before they get to the sea!" He had brought his divining arrows as was the pagan practice. Jabala shouted, "Surely sorcery is vain today," meaning that defeat was unavoidable. The Apostle, meanwhile, drew aside and showed remarkable bravery, standing his ground and calling on his companions, in the name of God, to rally around him and defeat the enemy. The 'Emigrants' and the 'Ansar' showed their habitual loyalty. Nearly a hundred gathered around him. 'Alí, as usual, showed singular courage and outstanding skill, killing the on-coming enemy left and right. Some were there who singly killed as many as twenty of the enemy that day. They turned the tables on the Hawazin. When the runaway Quray<u>sh</u> returned they found only prisoners, with hands tied, being led to the Apostle. Concerning this God revealed:

> Now hath God assisted you in many battlefields, and on the day of Hunayn when ye prided yourselves on your great numbers, but it availed you nothing, and the earth, with all its spaciousness was straitened for you: then turned ye your backs in flight. Then did God send down His spirit of repose upon His Apostle, and upon the believers, and He sent down His invisible hosts, and He punished the disbelievers. And such is the reward of the unbelievers.
>
> Q. 9: 25, 26

The enemy was routed. All who could, fled. The cavalry gave chase to the Thaqif who went toward Nakhla, many of whom were put to death. When the Prophet came to know that Khalid had killed a woman, He sent word to him forbidding the killing of women, children and hired slaves. He also ordered the captives and their possessions be taken to al-Ji'rana, a well about 24 km south of Makkah on the road to Ta'if.

The Prophet proceeded to Ta'if and laid siege to the city for some twenty days. The Thaqif and Hawazin who had retreated from Hunayn had taken refuge within the city walls shutting the gates and manning the walls with Archers. Fighting was severe and relentless but undecisive. After a few losses in life by arrows, the Prophet ordered the tents moved further away from the walls. Their attacks to make breaches in the walls resulted in more fatalities. The Prophet ordered their vineyards cut down. Then they broke camp and retired to Al-Ji'rana. While the siege continued, the Prophet received delegations from neighbouring tribes embracing Islám. On the day they left Thaqif one of his companions asked the Apostle to curse Thaqif, but instead he said, "O God, guide Thaqif and bring them to Islám."

At al-ji'rana, delegations arrived from Hawazin and accepted Islám. The Apostle's foster mother who had suckled him was of the Banu Sa'd, a Hawazin clan. He had spent six childhood years among them. They now appealed to the Prophet for leniency and favour. The Prophet returned their captive wives, children, camels and sheep and other possessions numbering some 6000 items. He also promised to return to Malik ibn 'Auf his family and possessions in addition to a hundred camels if he came to the Apostle as a Muslim. Now Malik had fled to Ta'if, and when he heard of the Prophet's promise, he escaped at night and joined the Messenger of God. His family and property were returned to him and he was given a hundred camels. He became an excellent Muslim and a faithful ally of the Muslims in fighting Thaqif, raiding their flocks and harassing them until they were in dire straits.

The Prophet's generosity in the division of spoils to a number of his former enemies in order to win them over and gain men's hearts to Islám by giving several of them 100 and 80 and 50 camels each as gifts of conciliation aroused the ire of the 'Helpers' of Madinah. When he heard of their murmurings and complaints, he had them assembled in an enclosure and addressed them saying: "O men of Ansar![108] What is this I hear of you? Do you think ill of me in your hearts? Did I not come to you when you were erring and God guided you; poor and God made you rich; enemies and God softened your hearts?" They answered, "Yes indeed, God and His Apostle are most kind and generous." He went on, "If you tell me what is in your heart — 'You came to us

---

[108] The original inhabitants of Madinah who helped the 'Emigrants' at the time of the Hijrah.

discredited and we believed you; deserted and we helped you; a fugitive and we took you in; Poor and we comforted you; you are no doubt telling the truth. But are you disturbed in mind because of the good things of this life by which I win over a people that they may become Muslims while I entrust you to your Islám? Are you not satisfied that men should take away flocks and herds while you take back with you the Apostle of God? By Him in Whose hand is the soul of Muhammad, had it not been for the 'Emigrants', I would have severed my tie with the Quraysh and would be one of the 'Ansar' myself. If all men went one way and the 'Ansar' another, I should take the way of the Ansar'. God have mercy on the 'Ansar' their sons and their sons' sons." The people wept until the tears ran down their beards, and said, "We are satisfied with the Apostle of God as our lot and portion." Then the Apostle went off and they dispersed. A total of 12 Muslims were martyred at the siege of al-Ta'if, seven from Quraysh, one from Banu Layth, and four from the Madinan 'Helpers'.

THE RAID ON TABUK, A.H. 9

Tabuk is a small town in the north of Hijaz, a short distance south of the present Jordan and east of the Gulf of 'Aqaba. The Apostle was informed that the Byzantine emperor had assembled a large army and was bent on the conquest of Madinah. He ordered his companions to make preparations for war and told them that they would march out to Tabuk. This was in the midst of a hot summer when people preferred to stay in the shade of their orchards and enjoy the ripe fruits, but in obedience to the Prophet's command, an army of 30,000 men was equipped at great cost and sacrifice. The rich Muslims, particularly 'Uthman, the Prophet's son-in-law, contributed liberally to this cause providing mounts, armour, weapons and provision. The hypocrites, 'Abdullah ibn Ubayy, Jadd and others found excuses to stay home. Jadd's excuse was that he was addicted to women and seeing Byzantine women would be a strong temptation for him. God revealed concerning them:

They formely sought to raise a sedition, and they disturbed thy affairs, until the truth came, and the decree of God was made manifest; although they were averse thereunto. There is of them who saith (unto thee), 'Give me leave (to stay behind), and expose me not to temptation'. Have they not fallen into temptation (at home)? But hell will surely encompass the unbelievers.

See also 9:81-83

Q. 9: 48, 49

But there were believers who were eager to join the army, but had no mounts or provisions, and the Apostle could not provide for them. They were known as The Weepers as in their helplessness they bemoaned their plight. Other more fortunate Muslims gave some of them mounts and some dates enabling to participate in the expedition[109].

---

[109] See 9: 92, 93

The Apostle left 'Alí in charge of their families, and set off. The hypocrites spread a rumour that 'Alí was a burden to the Apostle and he relieved himself of him. 'Alí seized his weapons, caught up with the force, and told the Prophet about the rumors the hypocrites were Spreading. The Prophet said, "They lie. I left you behind because of what I had left behind, so go back and represent me in my family and yours. Are you not content, 'Alí, to stand to me as Aaron stood to Moses, except that there will be no Prophet after me?" So 'Alí returned to Madinah.

At al-Hijr, the Prophet ordered the men not to drink any of its water, nor use it in their ablutions, nor in their doughs; and if any dough had been made with that water, the dough to be fed to the camels, and not baked into bread. The next morning men had no water and complained to the Apostle. He prayed. God sent a cloud and it rained so much that they and their mounts were satisfied and they carried away what they needed. Earlier a decision had taken place between two believers as to whether the men could recognize a hypocrite among them. One of them said that believers recognized hypocrisy even in brothers, fathers, uncles, but they covered it up. When the incident of the rain happened, a believer told a doubter "Woe to you! Have you anything more to say after this?" He said, "It is a passing cloud?"

One day the Apostle's camel was lost, and some went in search of it. Zayd of the Jewish tribe of al-Qaynuqa who had accepted Islám but was a hypocrite said mockingly, "Muhammad claims to be a Prophet in communication with heaven; how come he doesn't know where his camel is?" The Apostle said to 'Umara, a companion, "A man has said so and so (repeating Zayd's words but not mentioning his name); by God, I know only what God tells me and shows me. It is in this wadi in such and such a glen. A tree has caught it by its halter; so go and bring it to me." 'Umara brought the camel back and returned to his camp. He told his friend, "By God, what a wonderful thing the Messenger of God has just told us about something said by someone of which God has informed him;" and he repeated what the Apostle had reported. His friend said, "By God, it was Zayd who said those very words just before you came." Zayd's hypocricy was made clear and 'Umara severed his association with him.

The story of Abu Dharr, one of the Apostle's sincerest believers and the Prophet's prophecy about him is very interesting. While the troops marched, some lagged behind. The Apostle used to say: "Leave him, for if there is any good in him God will unite him with you, if not, God has relieved you of him." Then they reported to him that Abu Dharr had fallen behind, and he repeated the same statement. It so happened that Abu Dharr's camel was too weak to walk, so he packed his belongings and proceeded on foot following the trail of the troops. At a halting place, they spotted a man coming from a distance. The Prophet said that he wished it was Abu Darr, and when he came nearer they noticed that indeed it was Abu Dharr. The Messenger of God said, "May God have mercy on Abu Dharr! He walks alone, will die alone, and will be raised alone." Many years later, 'Uthman, the third Caliph, exiled Abu Dharr. He, his wife and a slave lived in a village three days' journey north of Madinah. When he died, there was no one to bury him. He had asked his wife to wash him, wrap him in a shroud, and leave him on the roadside. A caravan arrived and he was given a suitable burial. 'Abdullah ibn Masud, a member of the Caravan, remembered the Prophet's predictions about him made on the way to Tabuk, and wept over him.

When the Apostle reached Tabuk the governor of Aylah (now called 'Aqabah, the northernmost port of the Gulf of 'Aqabah on the Jordanian side), the people of Jarba' and Adhruh offered poll tax and signed treaties with him. He sent Khalid ibn al-Walid at the head of a small party to Ukaydir, the Christian king of Duma. He, his brother Hassan and a few members of his family armed with hunting spears came out hunting wild cows as was their wont. They encountered Khalid's group. Hassan was killed and Ukaydir was seized and brought to the Apostle of God. The Prophet spared his blood. He paid the poll-tax and made peace with him.

The Messenger of God spent ten nights in Tabuk and, being informed that the Byzantines had no intention of conquering Madinah and the reports that had reached him were false, returned to Madinah. A short distance from Madinah, some people who had built a mosque to lure the Apostle in for prayer intending to kill him, asked him to visit them and pray in the mosque. The Apostle, aware of their treacherous designs had it burnt down. God revealed concerning this matter:

> There are some who have built a temple to hurt the faithful and to propagate infidelity, and to foment division among the true believers, and for a lurking-place for him who hath fought against God and His Apostle in time past; and they swear, saying, 'Verily we intend no other than to do for the best': but God is witness that they do certainly lie. Stand not up to pray therein for ever.
>
> Q. 9: 107

When the Messenger of God returned to Madinah, he went straight to the mosque and said prayers. Then some eighty disaffected persons who had remained behind came to him with different excuses. He asked God's forgiveness for them. Among these were three who told him the truth. They had no excuse, but were heedless. They had been good Muslims with unblemished characters and were respected in the community; they were not of the hypocrites who had given the Messenger false excuse. God put these three to the test. His Apostle dismissed them and told the believers not to associate with them. For fifty days they remained virtually ostracised. No one talked to them. At the end of the fortieth day they were commanded to separate themselves from their wives, not to divorce them, but not to approach them. They suffered much but endured and accepted their punishment patiently until the Word of God was brought to them.

> And He is also reconciled unto the three who were left behind, so that the earth became too strait for them, notwithstanding its spaciousness, and their souls became straitened within them, and they considered that there was no refuge from God, otherwise than by having recourse unto Him. Then was He turned unto them that they might repent; for God is easy to be reconciled and merciful. O true believers, fear God, and be with the sincere.
>
> Q. 9: 118-119

Everyone was jubilant and congratulated them. Ka'b ibn Malik, the youngest of the three tells of his reception by the Apostle: "When I saluted the Apostle he said as his face shone with joy, 'This is the best day of your life. Good news to you!' I said, 'From you or from God?' 'From God, of course,' He said. When he had good news to tell his face glowed like the moon, and we used to recognize it." Ka'b then offered his property as alms of penitance to God and His Messenger. The Prophet asked him to keep some for himself. Then he said to the Messenger of God: "God has saved me through truthfulness, and part of my repentance towards God is that I will not speak anything but the truth so long as I live." Then he added, "From the day I told the Apostle that to the present day I never even purposed a lie, and I hope that God will preserve me for the rest of my days."

THE YEAR OF THE DEPUTATIONS
— A.H. 9

A deputation of the Banu Asad arrived, telling the Apostle that they had come on their own without being compelled to do so, although their real purpose was to seek material assistance in a year of famine.

Their manner was condescending as though they were doing the Apostle a favour by accepting Islám. God revealed concerning them:

They condsider thee to be beholden to them by their embracing Islám. Say: 'Do not count your embracing Islám as a favour to me; nay, rather God confers a favour upon you in that He has guided you to the faith.'

Q. 49: 17

A deputation also arrived from Bali

And yet a third came from the Dariyyun from Lakhm.

These came before the Apostle's expedition to Tabuk.

'Urwa ibn Mas'ud of the tribe of Thaqif was loved and obeyed by his people. When the siege of Ta'if was lifted and the Apostle was on His way back to Madinah, 'Urwa left Ta'if and hurried forth to catch up with him. He accepted Islám and asked to return to his people. "They will kill you," the Apostle told him. But 'Urwa said that the Thaqif held him dearer than their own children, so he expected no opposition from them. But things turned out differently. When his people learned he had become a Muslim, they attacked and killed him.

Thaqif, however, could not exist in isolation for long. Quraysh and Hawazin had become Muslims making their position precarious. They took counsel among themselves and decided to take the course taken by their neighbours — pay homage to the Apostle and accept Islám. They sent a delegation to Madinah which arrived after the Prophet's return from Tabuk. They submitted a number of conditions, among which were that Al-Lat, their idol, remain undestroyed for three years to appease the fanatics, and the women until they accepted Islám; that they may not be asked to destroy their idols with their own hands; and that they be freed from the obligation to pray. The Apostle could not accept the first condition and refused to set a specific time for its destruction, accepted the second condition and said about the third request, "There is no good in a religion which has no prayers." After arguing the points raised, they accepted Islám and received their document, fasting with the Apostle the remaining days of Ramadan. Abu Sufyan and al-Muqhira were delegated by the Apostle to accompany them back to Ta'if and to destroy al-Lat.

The occupation of Makkah and the surrender of Thaqif led the Bedouin Arab tribes to send deputations to Madinah to pay homage to the Apostle, to be recognized as Muslims and to be included in the greater community of Islám. They came in troops in fulfilment of God's promise to His Apostle:

When the assistance of God shall come, and the victory; and thou shalt see the people enter into the religion of God by troops: celebrate the praise of thy Lord, and ask pardon of Him; for He is inclined to forgive.

Q. Sura 110

A deputation came from Banu Tamim. These were bedouins ill-mannered, lacking in refinement. 'Uyayna and al-Aqra'[110] called out the Apostle rudely when he was resting

---

[110] These were two chiefs of the clans of Abu Tamin who were with the Apostle at Hunayn and at the siege of Ta'if. To each the Apostle had gifted a hundred camels — a conciliatory gesture.

at noon in his apartment. "Come out to us, Muhammad!" they shouted several times. The Apostle came out to them[111]. It was the custom among the Arabs in such ceremonial receptions, for their poets and orators to recite poems and read long orations in praise of God and their own greatness. In boastful and exaggerated speech the orator remarked that they were the strongest people, had the best equipped soldiery, had no equal among mankind, and so on and so forth. This was usually replied to by the host or someone he designated. The Apostle called on Thabit to reply. He praised the Lord and His choice from among mankind, Muhammad, honoured by noble lineage, whom He made truthful in speech and the recipient of His Revelation. He then spoke about the 'Emigrants' and the 'Helpers' who believed in God and His Apostle, rendered him help and support, and, finally, ended by saying: "These are my words and I ask God's pardon for myself and the believers both men and women. Peace be upon you." The poets then exchanged long poems. Al-Aqra' then said, "By my father, this man (meaning the Prophet) has a helper. Indeed, his orator and his poet are better than ours and their voices are louder than ours." Then they accepted Islám and the Apostle gave them gifts.

The Prophet received a letter from the kings of Himyar[112] in which they proclaimed their acceptance of Islám and rejection of polytheism. The Prophet wrote them a rather lengthy letter conveying to them their duties and obligations as Muslims - prayer, fasting, alms-giving, the Zakat, the

---

[111] God revealed concerning this: As to those who call unto thee from without the inner apartments; the greater part of them have no perception (of the respect due to thee).

[112] An Arab kingdom in the extreme southwest of the Peninsula. They ruled Yaman until they were conquered by Abyssinia. They sought the help of the Persian Sasanid kings to expel the Abyssinians. The Persians drove out the Abyssinians and made Yaman a satrapy, the Himyar king ruling together with a Persian Satrap. Badhan, the fifth Satrap, embraced Islám A.H. 6. Altogether three kings sent letters to the Apostle.

division of booty, the payment of the fifth as God's right. He also itemized the requirements of Zakat on landed property, on livestock and on other possessions. He stressed the need to help believers against polytheists and defined their relationship with Jews and Christians. He sent messengers to them to teach them the Qur'án and the precepts of Islám and to collect their dues as Zakat as well as alms.

Deputations came from Bahra. Banu al-Bakka', Banu Fazara, The'laba ibn Munqidh, Sa'd Hudhaym and a score of other Bedouin tribes, large and small, all declaring their acceptance of Islám and alliegance to the Prophet. Teachers and Qur'án reciters were sent to many tribes and the Apostle instructed them to deal gently with people, to avoid harshness, so as not to repel them and to teach them God's good news with kindness, truthfulness and sincerity.

Then in A.H. 10, Khalid ibn al-Walid commanded a contingent that was sent by the Apostle to Najran, a city mid-way between Yaman and Makkah, inhabited by a large Christian community as well as by polytheists, with instructions to invite them to Islám, to promise them safety if they accept, and fighting if they fail to accept within three days. They accepted and Khalid stayed with them and taught them the ordinances of Islám. Khalid reported the matter to the Apostle through a letter to which the Apostle replied inviting them to send a desputation to him. The deputation arrived in due course and testified to the oneness of God and Muhammad as His Servant and Apostle. When asked by the Apostle whom they praised, Khalid or him, they said, "Neither, we praise God who guided us through you." "You are right," the Apostle said.

The Apostle appointed Qays as their leader, and they returned to Najran. Some four months after their return the Apostle died.

'ALÍ PROCLAIMED THE DECLARATION OF IMMUNITY—A.H. 9

Historians record different reports regarding the pilgrimage of the year nine and the announcement of the Declaration of Immunity. However, the differences are on minor points. On the basic issue, no conflict of opinion exists. The Apostle appointed Abu Bakr to lead some 300 believers who wished to go on pilgrimage to Makkah. When they set out, he received a momentous Revelation from God concerning the future relationship between him and the idolatrous tribes who, with few exceptions, had broken their pacts with him and who could not be trusted to honour contractual agreements, i.e. they preferred the lawlessness and the feuds of pre-Islamic society. This divine command is embodied in Sura 9: 1 - 40.

The Apostle of God called 'Alí and instructed him to proclaim the Declaration publicly on the day of sacrifice when they would all be assembled at Mina. Someone suggested that the Declaration could be sent to Abu Bakr as leader of the Hajj, but the Prophet said, "None shall transmit it from me but a man of my own house." 'Alí caught up with the pilgrims and informed Abu Bakr of his own mission. "Have you come to give orders or to convey them." They then continued their journey to Makkah under the leadership of Abu Bakr.[113]

---

[113] The account so far has been from Ibn Ishaq's Sira. Tabari's version, reporting later accounts is that Abu Bakr returned to Madinah and said to the Prophet, "O Messenger of God, may you be ransomed with my father and mother! Was anyting revealed about me?" "No," He replied, "but no one except me or someone from my family should communicate the Declaration! Aren't you pleased, O Abu Bakr, that you were with me in the cave, and that you shall be my companion in the cistern?" Abu Bakr was comforted, returned and led the pilgrimage. This was a clear sign of the superior station of 'Alí over the other companions, but they failed to recognize it.

On the day of 'Arafat, 'Alí read to the congregation the entire Declaration, giving the polytheist tribes four months respite to repent and join the brotherhood of Islám or taste divine chastisement. "God is clear of the idolaters, and His Apostle also. Wherefore if ye repent, this will be better for you; but if ye turn back, know that ye shall not weaken God; and denounce unto those who believe not, a painful punishment." (Q. 9:3) "They will please you with their mouths, but their hearts will be averse from you; for the greater part of them are wicked doers ... And if, after concluding a covenant, they break their oaths, and revile your religion, then fight the leaders of disbelief, for no oaths is binding with them, that they may desist." (Q. 9:8, 12)

Those people who had specific contractual agreements with the Apostle were given respite to the end of their terms. No agreement was to be broken before the termination of its time. "So long as they behave with fidelity towards you, do ye also behave with fidelity towards them." (Q. 9:17)

"And if any of the idolators shall seek thy protection, grant him protection that he may hear the Word of God, and then let him reach his place of safety. This because they are people devoid of knowledge." (Q. 9:6)

"O true believers, verily the idolators are unclean; let them not therefore come near unto the Holy Mosque (Ka'ba) after this year." (Q. 9:28) See also Vs. 17-18.

Circumambulation of the Holy Mosque in the nude was also prohibited. This was customary among some polytheists in pre-Islamic days.

These were the main terms 'Alí pronounced to the pilgrims, both Muslim and polytheist, who were assembled at Mina.

THE FAREWELL PILGRIMAGE
—A.H. 10

The Apostle received a letter from Musaylimah of al-Yamamah, a district east of Makkah, a letter which read:

"From Musaylimah the Apostle of God to Muhammad the Apostle of God. Peace upon you. I have been made partner with you in authority. To us belongs half the land and to Quraysh half, but Quraysh are a hostile people."

Now Musaylimah was in the deputation of Banu Hanifah, all of whom accepted Islám, but when they returned to Yamamah, Musaylimah apostatized, and sent the above letter. The Messenger of God replied:

From Muhammad the Apostle of God to Musaylimah the liar. Peace be upon him who follows the guidance. Surely, the earth belongs to God who bequeatheth it to whom He will among His servants. The ultimate issue is to the God-fearing."

The Messenger of God sent representatives to the various tribes that had accepted Islám to collect dues. He himself prepared for pilgrimage, the last of his life, known as the Farewell Pilgrimage. All those who had brought beasts of sacrifices could participate in the rites. All others including his wives were barred from participation in the rites. The Apostle sacrificed a large number of beasts in his own name, and in the names of his wives to whom he sent of the meat.

'Alí returned from the expedition to Yaman and participated in the rites because he had taken an oath to do so. Since he had no sacrificial animal, the Apostle made him a partner in his. The rites of pilgrimage, as decreed and performed by him became the model of pilgrimage and the practice of the pilgrims to this day.

Salman who was among the Apostle's close companions in this Farewell Pilgrimage, has reported the following:

"When the rites of the pilgrimage had been accomplished, the Apostle entered the Ka'ba, then clutching the door ring with both hands, he turned his blessed face to the people and said, 'Do not you wish that I would tell you of the signs of the Hour?' I was nearest to him and said, 'Inform us, O Messenger of God!' He then said, 'Verily of the signs of the Hour are the abandonment of prayer, the pursuance of passion and desire, the love of pleasure, the reverence of the rich, and the purchase of mammon at the price of Faith.' Astonished, I asked, 'O Messenger of God! Will everything that you said truly happen?' 'Assuredly, by God in Whose grasp is my very soul!'[114]

On his way to Madinah, He stopped at a well, called Ghadir-Khumn and delivered another long sermon. He knew his end was fast approaching and he desired to give final counsels and injunctions to the believers. Concerning a momentous event which occured at this station on their journey, 'Abdu'l-Bahá wrote to a believer in reply to his question:

"You have asked concerning the Ghadir-i-Khumm: the story of the incident that took place there is this: during the Farewell Pilgrimage, at Ghadir-i-Khumm which is a station between Madinah and Makkah, the Messenger (i.e. Muhammad) held 'Alí by his waist

---

[114] Cited in vol. 2, pp. 711-12, 'Qamus-i-Iqán', by Ishraq Khavari, from 'Tafsir-i-Safi' by Mulla Muhsin Fayz-i-Kashani, under caption: 'For what do they (the infidels) wait, but the Hour come suddenly on them. Already are its signs come!' Q. 47:18 This sermon is quite lengthy. Only the above passage has been cited.

wrapper, raised him and said in a loud voice, 'O people! Whoever hath me as his Lord verily hath this 'Alí as his Lord. Then, He added, 'O God, succor whoever supports him and abandon whoever turns away from him; render victorious whoever assists him and defeat whoever forsakes him."

"All those present hailed and lauded Him. Even 'Umar raising his voice in praise, said, 'Excellent, excellent, O 'Alí, in truth you are my Lord and the Lord of all the believers, men and women.' However, later they forgot."[115]

The Messenger of God fell ill shortly after his return from Makkah. It is said that about a month before his passing, he had a number of his close companions gathered and said, "Welcome to you. May God treat you with compassion, shelter you, protect you, exalt you, benefit you, give you success, assist you, preserve you, and receive you (kindly)! I enjoin you to fear God and entrust you to Him. I appoint Him as successor over you and entrust you to Him. 'Verily I am to you (from Him) a warner and an announcer of good tidings.' (Q. 11:12) 'Rise not up against God' (Q. 44:19) in His land and among His creatures, for He has stated to me and to you: 'That is the mansion of the Hereafter, We give it to those who desire neither exaltation in the earth nor corruption. The future belongs to the pious.' (Q. 28:23) He stated: 'Is there not a place in Hell for the arrogant?' (Q, 36:60)

On two separate occasions, He asked for pen, paper, or a shoulder blade 'so that I may write a document for you and you will never go astray after me.' They thought he was in great pain and was delirious, so they did not obey him. It is also reported that He asked for 'Alí, but 'A'isha said, "I wish you had asked for Abu Bakr!" and Hafsa said, "I wish you had asked for 'Umar." So they all gathered around him. He

---

[115] Maidiy-i-Asmani vol. 2, p. 14; author's translation.

dismissed them all and said he would call for them when there was need to do so.

It is recounted that on Monday morning the Messenger came out for morning prayer. Having completed the prayer, he turned to the people and in a loud voice that could be heard outside, he said: "O people, the fire has been kindled and dissension (Fitan) has set in like segments of a dark night. By God, you cannot lay anything to my charge. I did not make anything lawful for you except what was made lawful by the Qur'án. I did not make anything unlawful for you except what was forbidden by the Qur'án."

He died that same Monday, 12th Rabi'l A.H. 11 (June 7, 632) at about midday the very day he had entered Madinah ten years earlier. Authorities differ regarding His age at the time of His death — sixty, sixty-three and sixty-five have been stated in different accounts. Regarding the date of His death, there is no doubt. His birth, however, has not been clearly ascertained. If he was born in A.D. 570, he would be sixty-two at the time of his passing; if he was born in A.D. 571, he would be sixty-one.

He was washed by 'Alí, his uncle al-'Abbas and two of his uncle's sons, Zayd's son and Shuqran a freedsman of the Apostle. He was washed with his clothes on his body resting on 'Alí's breast. He was buried the following day.

THE PRIVATE LIFE AND THE STATION OF THE MESSENGER OF GOD AND HIS PREDICTION OF THE FUTURE OF ISLÁM

We are now approaching the end of our journey through the life of Muhammad the Messenger of God and the Seal of the Prophets. His impeccable character, unquestioned integrity, and above all His unwavering faith in God's unity, overpowering might, justice and mercy, his unshakable confidence in his promise of final victory and his utter servitude to His every behest, enabled him to eradicate idolatry from the Arabian Peninsula, put an end to barbaric practices in that territory, substitute the brotherhood of Muslims for tribal loyalties and protection, and transform a society of marauders into a unified, well-organized people who, in the course of the next hundred years were able to destroy the Byzantine and the Persian Empires and rule over an Islamic Commonweatlh stretching from the Atlantic to the Pacific oceans.

This is a passage from his moving sermon to the believers in his farewell pilgrimage:

"O ye men! hearken unto my words and take ye them to heart! Know ye that every Moslem is a brother unto every other Moslem, and that ye are now one brotherhood. It is not legitimate for any one of you, therefore, to appropriate unto himself anything that belongs to his brother unless it is willingly given him by that brother."

Thus he put an end to tribal affiliation, colour and race prejudices, and other false loyalties while forbidding looting, plundering and foraging for booty.

Never had any single soul brought about such radical transmutation in human society in such a short time with such meagre material resources, and in the face of such relentless and stubborn resistance and active opposition. Such super human success could be attributed only to divine Will and God's assistance and intervention.

Muhammad lived a simple, modest life. Even in the last years of his life when he could have lived a princely life, he was often seen sitting on the floor mending his clothes or cobbling his shoes. Dates, camel's milk, and its products, barley bread and water were his staple diet which he and his household enjoyed in very moderate quantities. His house was made of clay, of the kind that can still be seen in villages in the east, with rooms opening into a court-yard, each room occupied by one of his wives.

He was accessible at all times to seekers who wished to learn about His teachings; to disputants, male and female, who came to him for arbitration; to them who came seeking God's decision concerning serious and trivial matters arising in the community and when Revelations descended regarding those matters, they were recited to secretaries who wrote them down on slates of white stone, skins of goats and sheep and ribs of palm leaves. These scattered Revelations were recited by the few who could read, and committed to memory.

Sir William Muir in his 'Life of Mahomet', portrays some of the Prophet's life habits and character which became models of social behaviour in Islamic communities until modernism and love of affluence seduced men to a different course. He quotes 'A'isha's[116] conversation with a believer who questioned her regarding the Prophet's daily routine: "He was a man just such as yourselves; he laughed often and smiled much." "But how would he occupy himself at home?"

---

[116] The Prophet's youngest wife; she was about eighteen when Muhammad passed away.

"Even as any of you occupy yourselves. He would mend his clothes and cobble his shoes. He used to help me in my household duties: but what he did oftenest was to sew. If he had the choice between two matters, he would choose the easiest so that no sin accrued therefrom. He never took revenge excepting where the honour of God was concerned. When angry with any person, he would say, 'What hath taken such a one that he should soil his forehead in the mud!'"

Muhammad was very meek and humble. He is reported to have said, "I sit at meals as a servant doeth, and I eat like a servant for I really am a servant." He often gave a ride to a passerby who would then sit behind Him on an ass. In a gathering of friends and followers he would sit silently by for a long time. When He spoke, he enunciated every word distinctly with a soft voice and slow pace.

He loathed lying, deceit, treachery and breach of contract more than anything else, and disassociated Himself from perpetrators of such evils until they repented.

We quote another portrayal of Muhammad's character, by another British writer of great renown, Thomas Carlyle:

"Muhammad was not a sensual man. We shall err widely if we consider this man as a common voluptuary intent mainly on base enjoyments — nay on enjoyments of any kind. His household was of the frugalest, his common diet barley bread and water; sometimes for months, there was not a fire once lighted on his hearth. They record with just pride that he would mend his own shoes and patch his own cloak. A poor, hard toiling, ill-provided man, careless of what vulgar men toil for. Not a bad man, I should say, something better in him than hunger of any sort — or those wild Arab men fighting and jostling three and twenty years at his hand, in close contact with him always, would not have reverenced him so! There were wild men bursting ever and anon into quarrel, into all kinds of fierce sincerity; without right, worth and manhood, no man could have commanded them. They called him prophet. You say? Why, he stood there face to face with them, bare, not enshrined in any mystery, visibly clouting his own cloak, cobbling his own shoes, fighting, counseling, ordering in the midst of them, they must have seen what kind of man he was let him be called what you like! No emperor with his dignity was obeyed as this man in a cloak of his own clouting. During three and twenty years of rough actual trial, I find something of a veritable hero necessary for that of itself."

The believers were warned in the Qur'án about the Last Day in numerous verses[117]:

There is no piety in turning your faces toward the east or toward the west, but he is pious who believeth in God and the Last Day....

Q. 2: 177

... whoever believeth in God and the Last Day and doth good deeds — they shall have no fear nor shall they grieve.

Q. 5: 69

... Serve God, and expect the Last Day;...

Q. 29: 36

Shortly before His death, the Apostle of God gave the believers clear signs of the Last Day in a rather lengthy sermon given at the end of his farewell pilgrimage. An authoritative Hadith[118] reported by Jabir ibn 'Abdullah Ansari, a prominent believer and a close companion of the Messenger of God relates that sermon, passages of which are quoted below.

---

[117] See 2: 8, 62, 126, 228, 232, 264; 3: 114; 4: 38, 39, 59, 136, 162; 9: 18, 19, 29, 44, 45, 99; 10: 10; 24: 2; 33: 21; 58: 22; 60: 6; 65: 2

[118] Quoted in the 'Fara'id', pp. 264-266 from Majlesi's Ghaybat Bihar al-Anwar under heading 'Chapter on Sings'.

"During the farewell pilgrimage I was in attendance on the Apostle of God, may God bless him and his family and grant them salvation. When the prescribed observances of the pilgrimage were ended, he returned to the Ka'bah to bid it farewell.

He clasped the knocker ring of the gate and called in a loud voice 'O people!' The people in the Mosque and those in the market assembled. Then He said, 'Listen to what I tell you of the events which will happen after me. Those of you who are present ought to convey what you see and hear to those who are absent.' He then wept aloud in such wise that many of the people fell into weeping. Then when He calmed down, He said: 'Know all of you, may God have mercy upon you, that, in very truth, you this day are like leaves without thorns. It shall be so for 140 years. Then for the following two hundred years, thorns, without leaves, until naught is seen in it (Islám) but kings who are despotic, the rich who are greedy, the learned who long for possessions, the poor who are liars, the sheik[119] who are adulterers, the young who are shameless and women who are frivolous.'

Then He wept again. Salman the Persian rose and said, 'O Messenger of God! Inform us, when will all this happen?' He replied, 'O Salman! When your learned men become few, your Qur'án reciters become extinct, your alms you fail to discharge, your reprehensible deeds you disclose openly, your voices you raise in the mosque, wordly riches you place over your heads and knowledge beneath your feet, lying becomes your ordinary conversation and backbiting your normal pastime, the unlawful becomes your spoil, your old have no compassion for your young and your young no

---

[119] Shaykh has many meanings: a tribe elder, a chief, ruler of a Sheykodom, title of a Moslem religious leader. Shaykh ul Islám is the Grand Mufti, etc. I have adopted the English usage to allow the reader to pick any of the meanings.

respect for your old[120] — at such a time God's curse shall descend upon you, wretchedness and misery shall befall you, and your religion shall remain amidst you a mere word on your lips. And when you have attained to these qualities, dread the 'red winds' (wholesale slaughter), or 'Maskh' (metamorphosis), or the raining of stones upon you. And this has been verified in the Book of God (i.e. the Qur'án): 'Say: He is able to send on you a punishment from above you or from under your feet, or to throw you into confusion of different sects, and to make some of you taste the violence of others. Observe how variously we show forth Our verses that peradventure they may understand.' "

Q. 6: 65

We conclude this brief tract on the personality and station of Muhammad by citing a tribute paid to him by Bahá'u'lláh:

"...The purpose is that all should know of a certainty that the seal of the Prophets (Muhammad) — may the souls of all else but Him be offered up for His sake — is without likeness, peer or partner in His own station. The Holy ones (The Imáms) — may the blessings of God be upon them — were created through the potency of His Word, and after Him they were the most learned and the most distinguished among the people and abide in the utmost station of servitude. The divine Essence, sanctified from every comparison and likeness, is established in the Prophet, and God's inmost Reality, exalted above any peer or partner, is manifested in Him. This is the station of true unity and veritable singleness. The followers of the previous Dispensation

---

120 Compare the above signs with those given by St. Paul, 2 Timothy 3: 1-7, concerning the Last Days. These signs have been discernible not only in Islamic communities, but all over the world for some time now; an unconcerned humanity is looking on confused and bewildered but heedless and lacking in understanding.

grieviously failed to acquire an adequate understanding of this station..."

Tablet of 'Isharaqat, cited in *'Writings of Bahá'u'lláh,*

p. 232

INDEX